PATTERNBUILDE

From Co-Authors Terence Craig, CEO, PatternBuilders and Mary Ludloff, Marketing, PatternBuilders

Why would two executives from a growing startup in the big data and analytics industry write a book on digital privacy? Well, in our business we deal with the issues of privacy every day as we support industries like financial services, retail, health care, and social media. So we've seen up close how the digital footprints we leave in our daily lives can be easily mashed up and, through expertise and technology, deliver startling accurate pictures of our behavior as well as increasingly accurate predictions of our future actions. Far more is known today about us as individuals than ever before. How organizations, businesses, and government agencies use this information to track and predict our behavior is becoming one of the fundamental issues of the 21st century.

As leaders in a company that provides tools to make this possible, it is important for us to understand the issues of privacy as it applies to big data sets, singularly and in aggregate. We must do what we can to make sure that the significant benefits of big data analytics are maximized (consumer choice, improved health care, protection from terrorism) while the negatives are minimized (lack of privacy, political suppression, genetic discrimination). Of course, we do this for the obvious moral reasons. But there are practical reasons as well: If we do not, we will lose the trust of the consumers, the very people that we rely on for much of our data. Or as Reid Hoffman put it at *South by Southwest*, companies should never "ambush their users."

Why do we spend so much time writing and blogging about digital privacy issues? As a company that is on the forefront of creating sophisticated tools to analyze digital data, we are acutely aware of the powerful technologies and techniques we—and others in our industry—are developing. Data is the life blood of our industry. If we do not make an effort to understand privacy concerns and bring self-regulation to the forefront, it will disappear under the twin forces of individual distrust and over-regulation. This is why we spend a lot of time thinking about what we can do to ensure that our tools and expertise are used in ways that are ethical and positive. The book is a way in which we can help our customers and the public be proactive about privacy issues which, in turn, keeps us all on the right path. We would like to continue the conversation with you. You can tweet us at *@terencecraig* or *@mludloff*, email us at *bigprivacy@patternbuilders.com*, or follow us on our blog—*Big Data Big Analytics* (http://blog.patternbuilders.com/). Hope to hear from you soon.

About PatternBuilders
We provide services and solutions that help organizations across industries understand and improve their operations through the analysis of large and dynamic data sets. If you have big data you need to analyze, we can help you derive big wins.

O'REILLY®
Strata
Making Data Work

Learn how to turn data into decisions.

From startups to the Fortune 500, smart companies are betting on data-driven insight, seizing the opportunities that are emerging from the convergence of four powerful trends:

- New methods of collecting, managing, and analyzing data

- Cloud computing that offers inexpensive storage and flexible, on-demand computing power for massive data sets

- Visualization techniques that turn complex data into images that tell a compelling story

- Tools that make the power of data available to anyone

Get control over big data and turn it into insight with O'Reilly's Strata offerings. Find the inspiration and information to create new products or revive existing ones, understand customer behavior, and get the data edge.

O'REILLY®

Visit oreilly.com/data to learn more.

Privacy and Big Data

Terence Craig and Mary E. Ludloff

O'REILLY®

Beijing · Cambridge · Farnham · Köln · Sebastopol · Tokyo

Privacy and Big Data

by Terence Craig and Mary E. Ludloff

Published by O'Reilly Media, Inc., 1005 Gravenstein Highway North, Sebastopol, CA 95472.

O'Reilly books may be purchased for educational, business, or sales promotional use. Online editions are also available for most titles (*http://my.safaribooksonline.com*). For more information, contact our corporate/institutional sales department: (800) 998-9938 or *corporate@oreilly.com*.

Editors: Mike Loukides and Meghan Blanchette	**Cover Designer:** Karen Montgomery
Production Editor: Jasmine Perez	**Interior Designer:** David Futato
	Illustrator: Robert Romano

ISBN: 978-1-449-30500-0

[LSI]

1316095121

Table of Contents

Preface

Conventions Used in This Book

The following typographical conventions are used in this book:

Italic
> Indicates new terms, URLs, email addresses, filenames, and file extensions.

Safari® Books Online

Safari Books Online is an on-demand digital library that lets you easily search over 7,500 technology and creative reference books and videos to find the answers you need quickly.

With a subscription, you can read any page and watch any video from our library online. Read books on your cell phone and mobile devices. Access new titles before they are available for print, and get exclusive access to manuscripts in development and post feedback for the authors. Copy and paste code samples, organize your favorites, download chapters, bookmark key sections, create notes, print out pages, and benefit from tons of other time-saving features.

O'Reilly Media has uploaded this book to the Safari Books Online service. To have full digital access to this book and others on similar topics from O'Reilly and other publishers, sign up for free at *http://my.safaribooksonline.com*.

How to Contact Us

Please address comments and questions concerning this book to the publisher:

> O'Reilly Media, Inc.
> 1005 Gravenstein Highway North
> Sebastopol, CA 95472
> 800-998-9938 (in the United States or Canada)
> 707-829-0515 (international or local)

707-829-0104 (fax)

We have a web page for this book, where we list errata, examples, and any additional information. You can access this page at:

http://www.oreilly.com/catalog/9781449305000

To comment or ask technical questions about this book, send email to:

bookquestions@oreilly.com

For more information about our books, courses, conferences, and news, see our website at *http://www.oreilly.com.*

Find us on Facebook: *http://facebook.com/oreilly*

Follow us on Twitter: *http://twitter.com/oreillymedia*

Watch us on YouTube: *http://www.youtube.com/oreillymedia*

Acknowledgments

We would not have been able to write this book without the help of many people.

We would like to thank our spouses for going beyond the call, putting up with us genteelly (if there is such a thing) yelling at each other, proofing, and sharing ideas. It goes without saying that startups have long grueling hours and when coupled with our writing weekends, we did not have much time for anything else. Our spouses bore the brunt of most of this and we are eternally grateful that we have chosen so well!

We would also like to thank Mike Loukides, Meghan Blanchette, and the entire O'Reilly crew for the opportunity and support. We especially appreciated the gentle prodding when we were a bit late with drafts which helped us to stay the course.

Our thanks to Natalie Fonseca, the co-founder and executive producer of Privacy Identity Innovation (PII). Her excellent conferences taught us much we didn't know about privacy and her unstinting support of the book has our heartfelt gratitude.

A number of friends and colleagues reviewed drafts of this book. We thank them all for their insights and comments. Without a doubt, they all helped to make the book better.

Enough said. This book is soup! Time for some cocktails on the deck!

In Terence's Own Words...

To my Mother, Father, and my beautiful wife: without you there, there is no me. To my adopted Russian Crew, with a special shout out to Slavik and Sasha; to Dr. B, Sujata, and Elan, every time I hear how success ruins people, I think how you guys are the exception to the rule, thanks for having my back; to my Texas and North Carolina family (you guys know who you are and I am running out of room); to all the employees, past and present, that have helped me build PatternBuilders and last, but certainly not least, to my co-author and dear friend, Mary, thanks for one of the most rewarding collaborations of my career.

It's Mary's Turn Now...

My thanks to my husband and sisters who picked up all of the slack and kept me laughing throughout this "labor of privacy" (wait, I meant love!). To my dearest cousin, thanks for reminding me why I should periodically take grammar refresher courses and for having such a keen eye (and yes, I should have given you more time!). To all my friends and family, thanks for putting up with my endless questions on all things related to privacy to gain a better understanding of different viewpoints. Finally, to my co-author and equally (see above) dear friend, Terence: "I could not have picked a better person to work with to write a book about a topic that is so nuanced and complicated. We had our contentious moments but we never lost sight of the big picture and that made, I believe, for a much better book!"

CHAPTER 1

The Perfect Storm

If, like us, you spent the last 20 years or so working in the high tech industry, you've had a bird's-eye view of the evolving data privacy debate. No matter where you fall on the privacy continuum—from a cavalier approach to how your data is being collected and used to a more cynical and, some might argue, paranoid view of the endless ways your information could be hijacked—it is safe to say that the stakes have never been higher.

There is a perfect storm brewing; a storm fueled by innovations that have altered how we talk and communicate with each other. Who could have predicted 20 years ago that the Internet would have an all-encompassing effect on our lives? Outside of sleeping, we are connected to the Web 24/7, using our laptops, phones, or iPads to check our email, read our favorite blogs, look for restaurants and jobs, read our friends' Facebook walls, buy books, transfer money, get directions, tweet and foursquare our locations, and organize protests against dictatorships from anywhere in the world. Welcome to the digital age.

Digital technology has created and nurtured a new world order where much that was impossible is now possible. We may not have personal jet packs or flying cars, but we do have video phones and combat drones. We may not yet inhabit the world George Orwell predicted in his dystopian novel, *1984*, a world in which there was no right to privacy and the government used surveillance and misinformation to control its citizens; however, our government has certainly used our personal information to its advantage, resulting in far more knowledge about us than even Orwell could have imagined.

Our world has changed; some might argue for the better and others for the worse. Today, we give away more information about ourselves and have more data collected and aggregated about us than any group in human history. Most of it we give away for simple convenience and the use of "free" or almost free services. Some of it is collected surreptitiously or through aggressive government action, such as the eight million requests (*http://www.wired.com/threatlevel/2009/12/gps-data/*) the U.S. Department of Justice made to Sprint in 2009 for subscriber locations via their GPS phones.

Our offline life is now online. We trade our personal information for online conveniences like ecommerce, instant communication, keeping in touch with hundreds of friends or business colleagues, networking with communities about things we care about, and even for the chance of romance. In exchange, we are marketed to. Our data is aggregated and segmented in all sorts of ways: by age, by sex, by income, by state or city or town, by likes, by sites we visit. We are grouped in terms of our behavior and these groups are rented or sold to advertisers who want to sell us things.

Much of the privacy debate is centered around, or so most pundits will tell you, behavioral targeting. In a recent study (*http://www.google.com/hostednews/afp/article/ALeqM5jm38cd0yGVDPXRO1_dohxoq__-rw*) conducted by U.C. Berkeley and the University of Pennsylvania, 66 percent of those surveyed said they did not want marketers to tailor advertisements to their interests. When participants were told how their activities were tracked, the disapproval rate climbed higher, to between 73 and 86 percent. In a recent survey by Opera Software (*http://www.opera.com/press/releases/2011/01/28/*), Americans said they were more fearful of online privacy violations than they were of terrorist attacks, personal bankruptcy, or home invasions.

The concept of targeted advertising is not new. Yes, today it is much easier to digitally track everything, sort through it, and make educated guesses about what we'll buy. But is more intrusive advertising something to be feared? It is when you consider that this same process can be used to make educated guesses about a wide range of activities. Security agencies can use it to profile possible terrorists, the IRS to identify possible fraudulent tax returns, law enforcement agencies to surveil possible criminal activities, credit card and loan companies to determine good and bad credit risks. While data, in itself, may be benign, how it is used can run the gamut from harmless to what some might call exceedingly harmful and others might call truly evil.

Data privacy is not a debate about how we are advertised to. It is a debate about the collection and use of our personal information from a commercial and political standpoint. By giving out our information for the convenience of products and services, we have also opened the door to far more intrusive monitoring by government agencies in the name of national, state, and local security. How we reached this point is the result of technological innovation and entrepreneurship. Where we go from here is up to us.

Through the Looking Glass

It all started in 1969, with the founding of ARPANET (*http://en.wikipedia.org/wiki/arpanet*) (Advanced Research Projects Agency Network), a network of geographically distributed computers designed to protect the flow of information between military installations. This laid the groundwork for the Internet (*http://en.wikipedia.org/wiki/internet*), a network of networks and now home to millions of private, public, government, business, and academic networks all linked together and carrying vast amounts of digital information.

Along the way, several inflection points occurred that would end up putting the Internet at the center of our professional and personal lives:

- **The Internet becomes a household word**. In 1990, Sir Tim Berners-Lee wrote the initial specification for the World Wide Web, and by 1993, Digital Equipment Corporation officially "opened" its first commercial website. The mid-1990s featured the introduction of web browsers and heralded increasing access to PCs, with two out of three employees and one in three households having access.

- **Shopping goes online**. eBay and Amazon got their starts in 1995 with a new business model directed solely at the online consumer. This set the stage for traditional brick and mortar businesses recasting themselves in the online world, as well as the emergence of new online-only businesses like Zappos (*http://www.zappos.com/*) and Netflix (*http://www.netflix.com/*).

- **Search goes mainstream and validates a powerful, new advertising model**. In 1998, Google, following search pioneers like Yahoo and Lycos, went live with a better search algorithm, as well as superior ad targeting mechanisms. This not only changed the way people searched for information, but perfected content-based and paid query-based (*http://digitalenterprise.org/models/models.html*) advertising models that resulted in Google's $8.44 billion in revenue in the fourth quarter of 2010 alone. It also produced the largest collection of data on individual behavior in history.

- **Social media sites take off**. In 2003, following struggling social network pioneer Friendster (now a social gaming site), MySpace went live and grew to become the most popular social network until Facebook overtook it. In 2004, the term social media was coined (first used by Chris Sharpley) and Facebook was launched. In 2005, YouTube went online, followed by Twitter in 2006. All of these sites (and more) produce vast amounts of digital data on individual behavior, the relationships between people (the idea of the personal social network) as well as their locations (from services like Foursquare).

- **The rise of personal devices**. In 1996, the Nokia 9000 Communicator became the first mobile phone with Internet connectivity. In 2001, Blackberry was launched, the first email-enabled mobile phone system. In 2007, Apple introduced the iPhone, which set the stage for a host of mobile web applications and businesses. By 2008, there were more mobile phones with Internet access than PCs. In 2010, tablet devices, led by the iPad, took the market by storm, with more applications churning out more data. Now, for the first time, a user's location is an integral component of the device itself. It is possible to know where someone is located at any time without them telling you.

- **Communication becomes instant**. AOL's Instant Messenger (IM) introduced real-time messaging in 1996, which reached a much broader personal and business audience with the introduction of Skype and Microsoft's MSN Messenger. The SMS (Short Message Service) protocol was developed in 1984, making it possible for mobile devices to send text messages; this is now the preferred method of communication for teenagers and young adults. It is estimated that there will be over 3.5 billion IM accounts by 2014 (*http://www.radicati.com/?p=5290*). Similar to social media sites, instant messages produce vast amounts of information, not only about individual users but also about the depth and quality of their relationships with other people and organizations—the all-important social graph.

Today, we operate in an always-on, digital world: We work online, we socialize online, we follow news and our favorite shows online, we file taxes online, we bank online, we may even gamble or pursue sexual interests online. And everything we do leaves a digital footprint, so much so that we had to give it a name: big data.

Welcome to the Big Data Age

Unless you've been asleep for the past few years, you've probably read about the amount of data generated by our digital universe. Phrases like "drowning in data," a "vast ocean of data," and "exponential data growth," have been invoked to try to capture its size. Why? Because it's almost too big to grasp, or as IDC Research put it (*http://www.emc.com/collateral/demos/microsites/idc-digital-universe/iview.htm*):

- In 2009, the digital universe grew 62 percent or almost 800,000 petabytes (think of each petabyte as a million gigabytes, which translates into a stack of DVDs reaching from the Earth to the moon and back).
- In 2010, it was projected to grow to 1.2 million (final counts are not in as of yet) petabytes (*http://en.wikipedia.org/wiki/petabytes*).
- By 2020, it is projected to be 44 times as big as it was in 2009 (those DVDs would be stacked up halfway to Mars).

But big data is not just about size. It's about the sheer number of data sources available, its different formats, and the fact that most of it is user generated: 70 percent of the digital universe (*http://www.emc.com/collateral/demos/microsites/idc-digital-universe/iview.htm*) is actually generated by all of us through email, Facebook, Twitter, LinkedIn, Flickr, YouTube; the list goes on and on. There are:

- One trillion unique URLs in Google's index and two billion Google searches every day.
- 70 million videos available on YouTube (and they are viewed 100 million times on a daily basis).
- 133 million blogs.
- More than 29 billion tweets (and three million are added every day).
- More than 500 million active Facebook users and they spend over 700 billion minutes per month on the site.

Add to that the growing number of publicly available data sources from federal, state, and local government agencies, academic and research institutions, geospatial data, economic data, census data; this list goes on as well. With all that data being digitally proliferated, maintaining one's privacy from government or commercial organizations is a difficult, if not impossible, task.

From Pieces of a Puzzle to a Complete Picture: The Future Is Now

While the amount of data about us has been increasing, so has the ability to look at and analyze it. We have gone from having little bits and pieces about us stored in lots of different places off- and online to having fully formed pictures of who we are. And it is all digitally captured and stored.

Historically, two things had held the science of data mining, predictive modeling, and exploratory analytics back: the inability to store enough data and the cost of the computer power to process it. Today, the costs of storage and processing power are dropping exponentially and seem likely to continue to do so. At the same time, there is an unprecedented aggregation of data about each one of us available in digital format. This makes it easy for organizations of all sizes, as well as government agencies, to find information about any individual as well as use analytic models to predict future behavior.

Far more is known about us than ever before and that information can be used to predict behavior of all kinds, including buying, political, or criminal behavior. This same information is also routinely used to create profiles that identify potential threats to domestic or international security which, in sufficiently repressive regimes, can be fatal for citizens that match a predictive model's high-risk profile, guilty or not.

Advertising as the Big Bad Wolf

Is behavioral advertising really the big bad wolf when it comes to our privacy? Certainly, the concept is not new. It is simply a way to predict, by your behavior, what service or product you might be interested in buying.

In the pre-digital days, there were companies that specialized in analyzing buying behavior, like AC Nielsen, and companies that "rented" out their customer list, segmented by income level, sex, marital status, buying behavior, etc. Chances are your mailbox, like ours, was stuffed with all kinds of offers and you seemed to get phone calls about buying or selling something every hour. Most likely, those offers were the result of information you gave to your bank, credit card company, grocery store, or as a magazine subscription holder. But the information was, to some extent, blind. Your name and address were rented, usually as part of a group, but the renter (the business or organization that bought the advertising) did not have that information until, and unless, you responded. If you did, you then became a part of that company's mailing list and they would begin to build their own profile about you. So, even then, there were multiple profiles of you in multiple lead or customer databases based on your behavior with a specific company or organization.

In the Internet age, if my website travels indicate that I love Hawaii (targeted behavior), then I would see ads for trips to Hawaii when I am surfing, whereas someone who loves Alaska would see ads for trips to Alaska. This is simply a more personalized version of online advertising. You get served up ads based on where you go and what you do because your behavior is being tracked, and from that behavior, assumptions are being made about you. Advertisers like this model because they are able to reach a more interested audience with ads that are more relevant to them, which means that they are able to sell more stuff.

The difference between then and now is that everything you do online can be captured digitally and then analyzed and tied back to you. Google tracks online behavior, demographics, and interests with an advertising cookie. Lots of companies track your behavior—mostly through cookies that you allow, knowingly or not, to be installed on your desktop or other personal device—and there's a whole bunch of companies, like eXelate (*http://exelate.com/new/*), that sell your information. But for the most part, this information does not identify you specifically. Rather, it puts you in a group of people with similar demographics and interests and that group is then "rented" to someone to advertise (online, of course) to.

However, instead of multiple profiles, it is fairly easy to pull them together to get a much better understanding of who you are and what you do. For example, Spokeo (*http://www.spokeo.com/*) aggregates publicly available information about you from phone books, social networks, marketing surveys, real estate listings, business websites, and government agencies. If you search on your name, you may be surprised to see information about precisely where you live (from Google Maps), how much you paid for your house and the property taxes for it (from government data sources), the name of your spouse (from government records), how many people live in your home (from census data), all your phone numbers (from online white pages), previous addresses and the cost of those homes, and (depending on how public your social media presence is) far more information than you might want anyone outside of your close circle of family and friends to know. Most of this information could be collected pre-Internet, but would have required a great deal of time and effort to visit the various agencies, fill out the forms, and often, pay a fee. Today, all it takes is entering your name, or anyone else's, into a field and clicking Submit.

And it's not just about cookies anymore. For example, public data that might contain personal information about you can be scraped (otherwise known as web scraping), collected, and analyzed. There's also a relatively new concept, location marketing, where you are served up ads based on your location (which is available from the GPS chip in your phone). So, if your GPS location indicates that you are near a specific store, you could receive ads or coupons specific to that store.

Depending on your point of view, the amount of data that can be collected about you from public and private sources can either be disturbing, or simply the price you pay for living in a digital world. After all, the sites you use—like Facebook, Twitter, LinkedIn, Google, Foursquare, fill in the blank—need a business model that ensures their lasting presence. The implicit transaction you have with any of the sites that you visit is this: for the value I receive from you, I give you something of value back. That value is your personal information, and that information is rented out to advertisers regularly. And since there is so much information about you, which makes it far easier and more lucrative to advertise to you, your personal information is now more precious than gold.

But here's the thing: in concept, there is nothing morally wrong about behavioral advertising as long as you, the consumer, are aware of it. If your personal data is collected and used solely for the purpose of advertising, its impact is pretty benign. The privacy debate isn't about behavioral advertising, it's about all the other less benign ways in which your data can be mined and used. If we, as consumers, continue to associate data privacy with advertising practices, we are ignoring a far bigger issue: who is using our data, why are they using our data, and how can we protect ourselves from privacy invasions when we don't even know who is watching us?

Big Brother and Big Data Around the World

Governments are increasingly investing in capturing and analyzing digital footprints to combat crime and terrorism, flashpoint words guaranteed to galvanize most citizens to rank security over privacy when debating this issue. After all, how can we argue for privacy if our way of life is at risk?

The United Kingdom uses digital video technology to track citizens and visitors. They have more than 1.85 million CCTV cameras installed (*http://www.securitynewsdesk .com/2011/03/01/only-1-8-million-cameras-in-uk-claims-acpo-lead-on-cctv/*), or one camera for every 32 people. Any person walking across London will be captured on camera hundreds of times a day. British authorities have considered banning (*http:// www.express.co.uk/posts/view/39622/ban-the-hood-for-goodban-the-hood-for-good ban-the-hood-for-goodban-the-hood-for-goodban-the-hood-for-goodban-the-hood-for -goodban-the-hood-for-goodban-the-hood-for-goodban-the-hood-for-goodban-the -hood-for-goodban-the-hood-for-goodban-the-hood-for-goodban-the-hood-for-goodban -the-hood-for-goodban-the-hood-for-goodban-the-hood-for-goodban-the-hood-for -goodban-the-hood-for-goodban-the-hood-for-goodban-the-hood-for-goodban-the -hood-for-goodban-the-hood-for-goodban-the-ho*) hooded sweatshirts to make this type of surveillance easier, as well as using artificial intelligence (*http://www.pcpro.co.uk/ news/208452/ai-could-power-next-gen-cctv-cameras*) programs to identify pre-crime behavior so that officers can be dispatched before a crime is committed.

In the United States, many law enforcement agencies heavily rely on data collection and analysis techniques. New York City police would enter a person's name, physical description, ID, and companions' names into a central database when they approached people in so-called "stop and frisk (*http://www.nyclu.org/news/nypd-stopped-record-number-of-innocent-new-yorkers-2010-new-stop-and-frisk-numbers-show*)" operations. In 2010, these operations, which did not require police officers to observe any criminal behavior before "stopping," were performed on over 590,000 mostly Black or Hispanic persons. Law enforcement is no longer allowed to keep a database on individuals caught up in these blatantly discriminatory "stop and frisks" because of a state law in 2009 which makes it illegal; however, the "stop and frisk" (and many other databases, including a CCTV video database of individuals who have not been accused of any crime) continue to play a major role in New York City's data and analytics intensive Real Time Crime Center (*http://www.nytimes.com/2010/02/18/nyregion/18tattoo.html*).

Monitoring technology is taking off across the United States. CCTV cameras are installed across highway systems to monitor the flow of traffic and at traffic lights to monitor stop light violations. It is now commonplace to receive traffic citations in the mail. Although the practice remains controversial and is often challenged on constitutional grounds, it appears to be here to stay. Digital event recorders (*http://www.slate.com/id/2087207/*) (aka black boxes in cars), similar to those on airplanes, are being used by law enforcement to assess fault in accidents. Rental car agencies use similar technology along with GPS recorders to assess fines for going too fast or taking a car on to dirt roads.

Depending on the circumstance, it appears that the U.S. government has differing views on the preservation of privacy in the digital age. Internationally, it sees privacy as a democratizing force. For example, the government has given grants to technology providers to ensure that social networking tools like Twitter and Facebook are secure and not easily disrupted. That way, these tools can be used more effectively by pro-democracy demonstrators in places like Syria, Tunisia, and Iran. Of course, those governments have been known to use these same tools to target enemies of the state and, during times of unrest, to cut off all access.

In matters deemed as domestic security, the U.S. government pushes for more access to personal information. For example, the U.S. Department of Justice recently argued that the continued safety and security of the United States was dependent on maintaining a clause in the misnamed Electronic Communications Privacy Act (*http://en.wikipedia.org/wiki/electronic_communications_privacy_act*) that allows warrantless searches of an individual's email if it is stored in a hosted service, such as Gmail or Hotmail, if it is older than six months old. Through the Patriot Act, law enforcement can request broad surveillance powers from a special court (*http://firstmonday.org/htbin/cgiwrap/bin/ojs/index.php/fm/article/view/1198/1118*), which has far lower standards than those required for probable cause. Under this act, all library records for an individual can be turned over without the individual's knowledge, as the request is considered secret.

While the U.S. Constitution does not specifically mention privacy, several amendments in the Bill of Rights have been held by the Supreme Court as penumbral rights of privacy (*http://plato.stanford.edu/entries/privacy/*). Since this is a controversial part of the law and we are not lawyers, we will stick with the safe statement that the legal definition of what is private and what is not may be unclear in the "real (non-digital) world" but when compared to the digital one, it seems crystal clear. In other words, our "right to privacy," both in the digital and non-digital worlds, is constantly changing. However, in the "real world" there are precedents that approach the legal standard of "settled law" (Stare decisis (*http://en.wikipedia.org/wiki/stare_decisis*)) but like the technologies that drive it, there is nothing remotely settled about privacy law in the digital world.

This is the fundamental question we are faced with: in the digital age, do we have a right to not be observed by our government? If so, where? On the Internet, at the library, in public places, in private business, on the highway, or peacefully demonstrating against a government? In 1759, Benjamin Franklin said, "They who can give up essential liberty to obtain a little temporary safety deserve neither liberty nor safety." The question of privacy versus security has always been a profoundly difficult one. But the easy access and aggregation of individuals' private digital data makes it far more complicated in this age of terrorism and weapons of mass destruction.

At the Crossroads: Privacy versus Security and Safety

In the digital age, is privacy, as Mark Zuckerberg famously suggested, outmoded? After all, if you have done nothing wrong, you have nothing to worry about. Of course, if you make that statement to anyone who has been racially or religiously profiled, you might be surprised at his reaction. We are at a crossroad: how much privacy are we willing to give up? How transparent do we want to be? How much do we want our government to watch us? How much risk, in terms of crime and terrorism, are we willing to accept as the price for our privacy? How do we measure that risk—and how do we know that by giving up a certain level of privacy we are safer?

If you share photos taken from your cell phone online, chances are the embedded GPS information that precisely indicates the location at which the photo was taken went with it. Maybe it was a photo of your children at school and maybe you didn't want just anyone to know where that school was located. If you were on a community site, maybe you shared how a family member was very ill. Now you are looking for health-care coverage and somehow, unknown to you, the insurance company has that information. Maybe you disabled GPS tracking on your phone so that your location would be unknown. Law enforcement can still locate you with it. Maybe you live in France, where your data is required to be stored for a year by Google, eBay, and countless other companies. The French authorities want access to it should you be investigated. Maybe you tweet. Now the location of your tweet can also be tracked. Maybe you are fomenting a revolution using Facebook. Maybe the government you are demonstrating against is using Facebook to watch you.

It is one thing to collect and track information about you with your permission. But many companies and organizations have violated that permission, assuming that you opt in so that you are forced to opt out, putting cookies on your desktop without your knowledge, using questionable practices to collect data about you, sharing your information when you've asked them not to. Technology has made snooping easy and it's difficult to keep up with what you need to do to protect yourself.

If you think that it's the government's job to protect you, think about this for a moment: in the U.S. alone there are over 30 federal statutes and over 100 state statutes that protect some aspect of privacy. The regulations are piecemeal and designed to protect you if an industry, through self-regulation, does not. There is a pending Internet Bill of Rights and a possible do-not-track system similar to the do-not-call list that governs telemarketers. There are also consumer privacy organizations and action groups and companies that have made a business out of protecting your privacy, such as TRUSTe (*http: //www.truste.com/*). Although the Internet is global, the privacy issue is not, so privacy laws and regulatory actions and bodies differ from country to country.

We live in a complicated world. There are privacy players, regulators, and stakeholders; all holding forth on the state of privacy today and whether you should be confident or afraid about what is happening. What has become lost is exactly what our "right to privacy" means:

- What assumptions can we make about the personal data we now share online?
- Who owns our data and what are they entitled to do with it?
- What regulations are in place to protect us in the U.S. and abroad?
- What forces are at play trying to shape data privacy laws and expectations?
- What are legitimate government uses of digital data in a democracy?
- What role should we, the consumer, play in all of this?

In 1597, Sir Francis Bacon said, "Knowledge is power." It was true then and it is still true now. The more informed we are about privacy in the age of big data, the more we can shape and affect data privacy policies, standards, and regulations. This is not a debate about advertising; it is a debate about how we balance privacy, security, and safety in an increasingly transparent and dangerous world.

Bibliography

1. Kim Zetter, "Feds 'Pinged' Sprint GPS Data 8 Million Times Over a Year," *Wired*, December 1, 2009, *http://www.wired.com/threatlevel/2009/12/gps-data/*

2. Cameron Chapman, "The History of the Internet in a Nutshell," Six Revisions, November 15, 2009, *http://sixrevisions.com/resources/the-history-of-the-internet-in -a-nutshell/*

3. Wikipedia, "Internet," *http://en.wikipedia.org/wiki/Internet*

4. Wikipedia, "AOL Instant Messenger," *http://en.wikipedia.org/wiki/AOL_Instant _Messenger*

5. Wikipedia, "SMS (Short Message Service)," *http://en.wikipedia.org/wiki/SMS*

6. Berkman Center for Internet and Society, Harvard University, "A History of Digital Data Creation," *http://cyber.law.harvard.edu/digitaldiscovery/timeline_files/frame.htm*

7. The Radicati Group, Inc., "Key Statistics for Email, Instant Messaging, Social Networking and Wireless Email," April 19, 2010, *http://www.radicati.com/?p=5290*

8. Pew Research Center, "Pew Internet and American Life Project, Internet Trend Data," *http://www.pewinternet.org/Static-Pages/Trend-Data/Online-Activites-Total.aspx*

9. Joseph Turow, Jennifer King, Chris Jay Hoofnagle, Amy Bleakley, Michael Hennessy, "Americans Reject Tailored Advertising and Three Activities that Enable It," September 29, 2009 *http://ssrn.com/abstract=1478214*

10. Opera Software Press Release, "Who's Watching You," January 28, 2011, *http://www.opera.com/press/releases/2011/01/28/*

11. Michael Rappa, "Business Models on the Web," Managing the Digital Enterprise, January 17, 2010, *http://digitalenterprise.org/models/models.html*

12. Google, "Google Announces Fourth Quarter and Fiscal Year 2010 Results and Management Changes," January 20, 2011, *http://investor.google.com/earnings/2010/Q4_google_earnings.html*

13. IDC Research, "The Digital Universe Decade," May 2010, *http://www.emc.com/collateral/demos/microsites/idc-digital-universe/iview.htm*

14. NOAA (National Oceanic and Atmospheric Administration), "Tsunamis May Telegraph Their Presence," January 19, 2010, *http://www.noaanews.noaa.gov/stories2010/20100119_tsunami.html*

15. Adam Singer, "49 Amazing Social Media, Web 2.0, and Internet Stats," The Future Buzz, January 12, 2009, *http://thefuturebuzz.com/2009/01/12/social-media-web-20-internet-numbers-stats/*

16. Facebook, "Press Room Statistics" *http://www.facebook.com/press/info.php?statistics*

17. Nathan Wolfe, Lucky Gunasekara, and Zachary Bogue, "Crunching Digital Data Can Help the World," CNN, February 2, 2011 *http://www.cnn.com/2011/OPINION/02/02/wolfe.gunasekara.bogue.data/*

18. Terri Wells, " Website Marketing: How and Why Behavioral Advertising Works," November 1, 2006, *http://www.seochat.com/c/a/Website-Marketing-Help/How-and-Why-Behavioral-Advertising-Works/*

19. Matt Drake, "Ban the Hood for Good," EXPRESS.co.uk, March 30, 2009, *http://www.express.co.uk/posts/view/39622/Ban-the-hood-for-good*

20. Stuart Turton, "AI Could Power Next-gen CCTV Cameras," PC PRO, June 25, 2008, *http://www.pcpro.co.uk/news/208452/ai-could-power-next-gen-cctv-cameras*

21. New York Civil Liberties Union, "NYPD Stopped Record Number of Innocent New Yorkers in 2010, New Stop-and-Frisk Numbers Show," February 23, 2011, *http://www.nyclu.org/news/nypd-stopped-record-number-of-innocent-new-yorkers -2010-new-stop-and-frisk-numbers-show*

22. Michael S. Schmidt, "Have a Tattoo or Walk With a Limp? The Police May Know," *New York Times*, February 17, 2010, *http://www.nytimes.com/2010/02/18/nyre gion/18tattoo.html?_r=1*

23. Wikipedia, "Electronic Communications Privacy Act," *http://en.wikipedia.org/ wiki/Electronic_Communications_Privacy_Act*

24. Mary Minow, "The USA PATRIOT Act and Patron Privacy on Library Internet Terminals," LLRX, February 15, 2002, *http://www.llrx.com/features/usapatriotact .htm*

25. Joan Starr, "Libraries and National Security: An Historical View," First Monday, December 6, 2004, *http://firstmonday.org/htbin/cgiwrap/bin/ojs/index.php/fm/arti cle/view/1198/1118*

26. Stanford Encyclopedia of Philosophy, "Privacy," September 18, 2006, *http://plato .stanford.edu/entries/privacy/*

27. Wikipedia, "Confrontation Clause," *http://en.wikipedia.org/wiki/Confrontation _Clause*

28. Wikipedia, "United States Bill of Rights," *http://en.wikipedia.org/wiki/United _States_Bill_of_Rights*

29. Wikipedia, "NSA Warrantless Surveillance Controversy," *http://en.wikipedia.org/ wiki/NSA_warrantless_surveillance_controversy*

30. Wikipedia, "President's Surveillance Program," *http://en.wikipedia.org/wiki/Presi dent%27s_Surveillance_Program*

31. Unclassified Report on the President's Surveillance Program, July 10, 2009 *http:// www.scribd.com/doc/17267628/Unclassified-Report-on-the-Presidents-Surveil lance-Program*

32. USA Today, "NSA Has Massive Database of Americans' Phone Calls," May 11, 2006 *http://www.usatoday.com/news/washington/2006-05-10-nsa_x.htm*

33. Philadelphia Independent Media Center, "Why We Should Be VERY WORRIED about How Bradley Manning Is Being Treated," March 15, 2011, *http://www.phil lyimc.org/en/why-we-should-be-very-worried-about-how-bradley-manning-being -treated*

34. Mobile Marketer, "Location-based Marketing Can Increase Average Order Value, Frequency, Loyalty," Dan Butcher, March 29, 2011 *http://www.mobilemarketer .com/cms/news/q-and-a.html*

35. Fast Company, "Google, eBay, and Facebook Take on France Over User Privacy," Austin Carr, April 5, 2011, *http://www.fastcompany.com/1744794/google-ebay -facebook-take-on-france-over-privacy*

36. Managing the Digital Universe, "Data Privacy," Michael Rappa, January 17, 2010 *http://digitalenterprise.org/privacy/privacy.html*

37. The Wall Street Journal, "Proposed Bill Would Put Curbs on Data Gathering," Julia Angwin, March 10, 2011, *http://online.wsj.com/article/ SB10001424052748704629104576190911145462284.html?mod=e2tw*

38. ReadWriteWeb, "What Twitter's New Geolocation Makes Possible," Marshall Kirkpatrick, November 19, 2009, *http://www.readwriteweb.com/archives/twitter _location_api_possible_uses.php*

CHAPTER 2

The Right to Privacy in the Digital Age

Although the digital age we now live in has certainly raised the stakes on what is possible for governments, organizations of all kinds, and businesses to find out about us, the concept of privacy has always been around. We have argued about privacy, redefined what it means to be private, been fearful or cavalier about perceived privacy erosions, and sounded death knells for the end of privacy as we know it. Webster's (*http://www .merriam-webster.com/dictionary/privacy*) defines privacy as "the quality or state of being apart from company or observation" and one's right to privacy as "freedom from intrusion." How can a simple concept provoke such heated debate?

Perhaps the answer lies in the simplicity itself as it allows each one of us to interpret what it means to be private and that interpretation is shaped by available technology, our culture, history, and worldview. One cannot discuss privacy without also considering context. And what is contextually important to you may not be important to me. For example, I might object to Google Maps having an image of my home but you would only care if your child is visible in the image. We both believe that Google Maps makes our lives easier, the real issue is: what level of privacy are we willing to give up for that convenience? In this, as in most things, context is everything.

It's not surprising that culture plays a pivotal role in our perception of privacy. Topless sunbathing may be de rigueur on the French Riviera (or practically anywhere else in Europe) but it will get you arrested in the U.S. In contrast, we Americans think nothing of discussing how much our homes cost or how much money we "make" while Europeans are appalled at our crassness for discussing such private matters.

Is it so surprising, then, that any discussion of privacy can provoke opposing, and often polarizing, views? Our perception of privacy is informed by society, politics, our family, and our friends. The ongoing privacy debate we all, in some form or another, participate in is often framed by our views on morality and safety. How much privacy are we willing to cede to be safe (from criminals or terrorists or simply someone or something that might harm us)? It follows that privacy is never a simple discussion of right and wrong but a nuanced one that must balance opposing views to determine a course of action. So before we take a look at the regulatory state of play across the world (Chapter 3), let's consider what privacy encompasses, how our privacy norms have been shaped in the U.S. and abroad, the tension between privacy and other freedoms (or lack thereof), and how, for those of us who fully participate in all the digital age has to offer, it may very well be the end of privacy as we know it.

What Does Privacy Mean in the Digital Age?

What does privacy mean to you? If you are Jewish living in an anti-Semitic society, it might be your religion. If you are a human rights activist living in a dictatorship, it might be your political writings. If you are a philandering husband, it could be your emails and your physical location. If you are a police officer, it might be your home address. If you are a job applicant, it might be your arrest record. As individuals, we often judge privacy by the perceived harm that may occur if certain knowledge becomes public. Could we be embarrassed by this information, discriminated against, or our reputation (personally or professionally) damaged? Could our family or ourselves be hurt or killed? Or is privacy simply the information we deem private because it is no one's business but our own?

Typically, privacy can be categorized into three basic types:

- **Physical privacy**—or freedom of intrusion into your physical person, possessions, or space. Most countries have privacy laws that address unlawful search and seizures on your person or possessions.

- **Informational privacy**—your expectation of privacy when personal information is collected, stored, and shared in digital or some other format. Most countries have laws regarding the privacy of financial, medical, and Internet information to some degree.

- **Organizational privacy**—government agencies, organizations, and businesses expect to be able to keep activities or secrets from being revealed to others. For example, companies may expect to keep trade secrets and governments may choose not to reveal security policies to prevent terrorism (such as "secrecy" that is codified in the U.S. PATRIOT Act).

While individually, we have expectations of privacy, the digital age has certainly made significant in-roads into what we deem private and what may now be considered public:

- **Privacy of our communications**—most of us used to believe that our emails, phone calls, IMs, and in-person conversations were private. However, data retention policies, technology, legislation in many countries, along with the rise of new devices that enable constant communication surveillance have made communication privacy dependant more on a lack of interest in our personal communications rather than in the difficulty of monitoring them.

- **Privacy of our behavior**—before the digital age, our behavior within and without our homes in terms of how we acted, what we bought, where we went, and what we did when we got there was difficult to chronicle and share. Today, much of our behavior can be digitally captured and then used to predict what we'll buy or whether we fit a specific behavioral model that would indicate whether we are a good credit or insurance risk or conversely, whether we fit the profile for potential criminal or terrorist acts. That same digital profile can also be used to predict the most effective way to influence our behavior.

- **Privacy of our person—** our right to remain relatively anonymous in society if we choose, in terms of our likeness and whereabouts at any given point of time in a day, has certainly changed with the proliferation of closed circuit cameras, digital photos (along with the ability to digitally recognize faces using Facebook's facial recognition feature (*http://abcnews.go.com/technology/facebook-facial-recognition -feature-raises-eyebrows/story?id=13792666*) or others) and location tracking.

When we discuss privacy, we often cross categories and boundaries without realizing it. In the case of Google Maps as previously described, I may feel that my expectation of physical (my home has been violated) and informational privacy (a digital photo of my home and child are publicly accessible) has been violated, which has impacted my right to remain anonymous (privacy of person). In reality, a simple discussion of how Google Maps violated my privacy has many layers.

A similar case can be made for data protection and data retention policies and laws. They are related concepts but are often discussed together as a singular item. Data protections laws are designed to protect offline and online personal information, informational privacy. Data retention laws govern how long data, including personal information, must be retained by an entity for legal and business purposes. Both can have an impact on the privacy of communications, behavior, and person, but in different ways. For example, the protection of data keeps it secure (private) whereas the required retention of data, like emails, texts, and IMs, severely impacts the expectation of private communications. And as with all regulations, its utility is limited by the willingness of individuals and organizations to follow it. To borrow a line from the pro-gun lobby: "Computers don't breach privacy – people do!"

Underlying all of this is how we attach value to what we perceive as a violation of privacy. "What's the harm" is a common refrain in almost any privacy discussion because, particularly in the U.S., the danger that can be quantifiably shown dictates the level of response. For example, identity theft is a common risk to personal information violations. These violations may occur due to computer hacking, poor corporate and organization data security policies, or by individuals who simply impart too much information about themselves. Although these items are often classified as data security issues, they are also part of the larger privacy debate as data security breaches can lead to privacy violations. In these instances, the harm can be substantial in terms of financial loss which is why almost every country in the world has passed and enforced data security (or protection) laws and policies.

Of course our expectations of privacy and perceived harms are also driven by our history, culture, and society which, in turn, shapes those expectations. This results in what can only be characterized as divergent views and expectations of privacy with equally divergent bodies of laws and regulations that enforce privacy and assign harm. The American and European views of privacy certainly illustrate this divergence. While neither view is good or bad, there is a classic contrast between the two.

Privacy in the U.S.: The Right to Be Let Alone

In the U.S. Constitution, the word privacy is never mentioned. However, four Amendments (the first, fourth, fifth, and ninth, all a part of the Bill of Rights (*http://www .ushistory.org/documents/amendments.htm*)) are often cited to support the concept of the right to privacy (held by the Supreme Court penumbral rights of privacy (*http:// plato.stanford.edu/entries/privacy/*)). When it comes to privacy, the Fourth Amendment is the one that we are all most familiar with:

> "The right of the people to be secure in their persons, houses, papers, and effects, against
> unreasonable searches and seizures, shall not be violated, and no Warrants shall issue,
> but upon probable cause, supported by Oath or affirmation, and particularly describing
> the place to be searched, and the persons or things to be seized."[1]

In general, the American view of privacy is focused on the home and on the person. Our home and person is protected against intrusions (such as unlawful search and seizures, forced drug and blood tests, and pat downs), especially from the government. Outside of it, one might argue, we have very few expectations of privacy.

The concept of a right to privacy (*http://groups.csail.mit.edu/mac/classes/6.805/articles/ privacy/privacy_brand_warr2.html*) was first raised by Samuel Warren and Louis Brandeis in 1890 in an article for the Harvard Law Review. In it, Warren and Brandeis made the case for an individual's right to be let alone (widely quoted in many privacy discussions). Specifically:

> "These considerations lead to the conclusion that the protection afforded to thoughts,
> sentiments, and emotions, expressed through the medium of writing or of the arts, so far
> as it consists in preventing publication, is merely an instance of the enforcement of the
> more general right of the individual to be let alone."[2]

What is often forgotten is that Warren and Brandeis argued this concept as a rebuttal to such technological inventions as newspapers and photography where the personal details of one's private life were publicly disseminated (and where news stories were overdramatized and altered to fit story ideas designed to sell more papers—does that sound familiar?). In their view, although privacy was a part of common law (*http://en .wikipedia.org/wiki/common_law*), these technology advances made the case for an ex-

---

1. U.S. Constitution, Amendment 4, Ratified December 15, 1791

2. Samuel Warren & Louis Brandeis, Harvard Law Review, "The Right to Privacy," Volume 4, Number 5, December 15, 1980

plicit tort law, similar to those regarding slander and libel, where the difference between what is private and what is public would be legally defined. This laid the foundation for the U.S. concept of a right to privacy, which is commonly defined as "control over information about oneself."

As is so often the case, technology advances pushed the boundaries of privacy and what it meant to have one's privacy invaded. The census, development of the camera, printing press, telegraph, telephone, computers, Internet, and digital devices, all contributed to the American view of a right to privacy via the federal and state courts under tort law (*http://plato.stanford.edu/entries/tort-theories/*) as well as through a multitude of federal and state privacy-related statutes (covered in some detail in Chapter 3).

In 1960, William Prosser, a leading tort legal scholar, surveyed all the privacy-related common law tort cases (more than 300) and proceeded to categorize them into four types of intrusions, now collectively known as the four privacy torts:[3]

1. Intrusion upon the plaintiff's seclusion or solitude, or into his private affairs.
2. Public disclosure of embarrassing private facts about the plaintiff.
3. Publicity which places the plaintiff in a false light in the public eye.
4. Appropriation, for the defendant's advantage, of the plaintiff's name or likeness.

In so doing, Prosser narrowed Warren's and Brandeis' "right to be let alone" choosing to focus instead on these four rules and the harm (whether it was emotional, reputational, or some other injury) inflicted. The four privacy torts are the standard by which privacy violations are determined in the American judicial system. Many legal scholars and privacy advocates argue that the standard is far too rigid when dealing with privacy issues in the digital age. Certainly, we are seeing increasing legislative action, such as the recently introduced Privacy Online Bill of Rights (*http://www.govtrack.us/congress/ bill.xpd?bill=s112-799*), that attempt to define the boundaries on the collection and use of individuals' personal information.

In general, throughout American history, privacy discussions often revolve around the First Amendment (*http://www.usconstitution.net/const.html#am1*), which expressly grants the freedoms of religion, press, and expression, as well as the value and preservation of a free market system (*http://en.wikipedia.org/wiki/free_market*). We are most concerned about limiting federal and state powers and view our freedoms as a check on these institutions. Put simply, the U.S. system weighs privacy issues through a liberty and free market filter.

Privacy in Europe: Honor and Dignity

Ratified in 1953, the European Convention on Human Rights (*http://en.wikipedia.org/ wiki/european_convention_on_human_rights*) (ECHR) explicitly supports a right to

---

3. William L. Prosser, California Law Review, "Privacy," Volume 48, Number 3, August 1960, pg. 389

privacy: "Everyone has the right to respect for his private and family life, his home, and his correspondence."[4] Prior to this, many countries enacted privacy laws with explicit rights to privacy included in their constitutions (most focused on rights to privacy in the home and for communications).

The European concept of a right to privacy is centered round preserving the individual's honor and dignity in the public sphere. This idea can be traced back to ancient Rome (in the Law of Obligations (*http://en.wikipedia.org/wiki/law_of_obligations*)) classic Greece, and the medieval period which recognized that an individual had a right to be protected from interests that could cause an action for iniuria:

> "Because the action for iniuria was designed to protect honor and dignity, husbands could recover for insults to their wives, and fathers for insults to their children... And because the action 'rested on outraged feeling, not on economic loss' ... the penalty was measured according to the position of the parties, and the grossness of the outrage."[5]

What exactly does this mean? In the European view, individuals have the right to respect and personal dignity even in the public sphere. In other words, one should have control over one's own information and when and how it is disclosed publicly; in public, one should be treated with respect. The best example of this can be found in hate laws, legislation that criminalizes "speech that is *merely* deemed insulting to one's race, ethnicity, religion, or nationality."[6] Germany, Austria, Belgium, Sweden, Norway, France, and Britain have some type of hate speech legislation. One would be tempted to point to World War II and the rise of Fascism as the drivers of this type of legislation (and it certainly had an impact) but the seeds were planted long before that.

The history of honor and dignity can be traced back to the seventeenth and eighteenth centuries:

> "In earlier centuries, though, only persons of high social status could expect their right to respect to be protected in court. Indeed, well into the twentieth century, only high-status persons could expect to be treated respectfully in the daily life of Germany or France, and only high-status persons could expect their 'personal honor' to be protected in continental courts."[7]

The European tradition and expectations of privacy can be traced back to a time where one's status dictated how one would be treated: if you were of high class your honor (or dignity) must be respected but this same distinction did not, of course, apply to those in the lower classes. Although a semblance of class still exists in some European

---

4. Council of Europe, "The European Convention on Human Rights and its Five Protocols," November 4, 1950, Section 1, Article 8

5. Professor Ruth Walden, "Insult Laws: An Insult to Press Freedom," University of North Carolina, Published by the World Press Freedom Committee Rex Rand Fund, 2000, page 17

6. The Legal Project, "European Hate Speech Laws (*http://www.legal-project.org/issues/european-hate-speech-laws*)"

7. James Q. Whitman, Ford Foundation Professor of Comparative and Foreign Law, Yale University, "The Two Western Cultures of Privacy: Dignity Versus Liberty," April 1, 2004, Page 1166

countries, over time the right to honor and dignity was pushed down and out to encompass all citizens:

> "This long-term secular leveling-up tendency has shaped continental law in a very fundamental way. [For example] contemporary continental hate speech protections... can be traced back to dueling law."[8]

The same case can be made for prisoners. In the eighteenth century, your status determined your punishment. For example, if you were executed and of high status, you were beheaded; if you were executed and of low status, you were hanged. High-status prisoners were afforded comfortable accommodations while low-status prisoners were treated far more severely. Today, all prisoners are treated in the same manner (we are talking about Europe here and not about the special jail cells for celebrities (*https://www.prisonlegalnews.org/displayarticle.aspx?articleid=22532*) in LA County) and not surprisingly, the rights afforded to them are ones of respect and dignity.

There is no better example of the very different cultural views on what is private and what is not than the "public" arrest of IMF's chief, Dominique Strauss-Kahn, in New York City on charges of attempted rape. That produced:

> "...an earthquake of shock, outrage, disbelief and embarrassment throughout France on Sunday. Though horrified by those alleged crimes, the French press and political elite on Monday seemed perhaps more scandalized still by the images of Strauss-Kahn's brusque treatment by the New York police, and his exposure in the American media."[9]

In the European view, the media and other agents can endanger one's public dignity and should be restrained from doing so. Unlike the American system where one's freedoms are valued above all things and must be protected at all costs even at the risk of a loss of privacy, the European system puts checks on those freedoms in order to preserve one's expectation of privacy, even in public.

When comparing American's and European's view of privacy, one is tempted to boil it down to one of liberty versus public dignity. But as with any generalization, there are exceptions and even convergence. For example, the U.S.'s Health Information and Portability Accountability Act (*http://www.hhs.gov/ocr/privacy/hipaa/understanding/index.html*) (HIPAA) that protects private health information held by "covered entities" is considered to be the gold standard for privacy in the health care industry worldwide. Certainly, in this case both views hold that privacy should be sacrosanct. That being said, when you look at the regulatory states of privacy in the U.S. and Europe (Chapter 3) it is equally clear that the ways in which these two regions define and seek to enforce privacy infringements is very different.

---

8. James Q. Whitman, Ford Foundation Professor of Comparative and Foreign Law, Yale University, "The Two Western Cultures of Privacy: Dignity Versus Liberty," April 1, 2004, Page 1166

9. Scott Sayare, Maia De La Baume, and Robert Mackey, New York Times, "French Shocked by I.M.F. Chief's Perp Walk (*http://thelede.blogs.nytimes.com/2011/05/16/french-shocked-by-i-m-f-chiefs-perp-walk/*)," May 16, 2011

Privacy is Always Viewed through Some Sort of Prism

The differences between the American and European views on privacy can be extended to any region or country. How we view and value privacy is dependent on a host of influences that include our history, culture, and social norms. Added to that, age, ethnicity, and sex may influence our expectation of privacy. Those who live under repressive regimes, like China, Russia, or Syria, have no expectation of privacy. Teenagers also have no expectation of privacy. However, it is not outside forces that they fear intrusions from, but rather their parents. Those who live under democratic regimes have very different views of privacy. Is it any wonder that a right to privacy is so difficult to define?

Many privacy advocates argue for a universal right to privacy similar to the U.N.'s Declaration of Human Rights (1948) where:

> "No one shall be subjected to arbitrary interference with his privacy, family, home or correspondence, nor to attacks upon his honour and reputation. Everyone has the right to protection of the law against such interference or attacks."[10]

In this case, it seems that both the American and European views of privacy are given equal weight. But as we've discussed in this chapter and will go into far more detail in subsequent chapters, these two views can spawn divergent privacy laws and policies. Even within each view, there are contentious debates about what privacy means and the ways in which privacy can and should be enforced.

Privacy Without Borders

The digital age has added even more complexity to the privacy debate. In its truest sense, data has no borders. When we are traveling abroad, we must follow the laws and norms of the country we are visiting. We understand, implicitly, that if we run afoul of the "law" we will be subject to that country's judicial system. When we buy a home, we adhere to that country's or state's rules and regulations for real estate purchases. If we set up a business in one state, we understand that the process, policies, licenses, and permits may not be the same for another state or another country. What we do offline is governed by geographical borders. What we do online is not.

Data, in and of itself, has no country, respects no law, and travels freely across borders. It can be housed in a "cloud," physically located in any country in the world. It can be retrieved in a split second from anywhere. It can be copied—nearly 80 percent of enterprises around the world's stored data is duplicate information.[11] It can be retained

---

10. United Nations, The Universal Declaration of Human Rights (*http://www.un.org/en/documents/udhr/*), Article 12, December 10, 1948

11. McKinsey Global Institute, "Big data: The next frontier for innovation, competition, and productivity (*http://www.mckinsey.com/mgi/publications/big_data/pdfs/mgi_big_data_full_report.pdf*)," June 2011, pg. 19

forever. Unlike its offline counterpart, it can be subject to more than one set of laws and regulations. The best example of this may be the recent admission made by Microsoft (*http://www.engadget.com/2011/07/06/microsofts-patriot-act-admission-has-the-eu-up-in-arms/*) that data stored on its European servers can be handed over to American investigators without informing the individual in adherence with the U.S. Patriot Act. This is a violation of the EU's Data Protection Directive and Safe Harbor agreement (see Chapter 3) with the U.S. In this case, the Patriot Act trumps all other privacy legislation, regardless of where the data originated or where it resides.

It is possible to have privacy without borders? To develop one set of guidelines and governance for online data privacy that all countries could agree to? It certainly is a possibility—one that we will be looking at in Chapter 3. (But even if we could, how would we guarantee strict adherence to such a law?)

A Clash of Values

As we've already said, our expectation of privacy, how we define and value it is influenced by pretty much everything in our lives. For one country or region, a specific law regarding privacy may make perfect sense. For another country, it may be something else entirely. Often, an expectation of privacy is offset against other rights. For example, while European hate crime laws may be viewed as a form of honor and respect for your race or religion, someone else might argue that it is a form of censorship that infringes upon free speech:

> "... three disturbing trends now underway in Europe together represent the greatest erosion of democratic practice in the world's advanced democracies since 1945. First, anti-Nazi laws are being adopted in places where neo-Nazism poses no serious threat. Second, speech laws have been dramatically expanded to sanction speech that incites hatred against groups based on their religion, race, ethnicity, or several other characteristics. Third, these incitement laws are being interpreted so loosely that they chill not just extremist views but mainstream ones too. The result is a serious distortion and impoverishment of political debate." [12]

The right to be anonymous may come into play if your private information is revealed by the media to propel a story. Governments can compel companies or organizations to give them user information or can try and hack that information if they meet with resistance:

> "Google and Beijing had a well-publicized standoff starting in January 2010, following revelations of a large-scale, sophisticated computer exploitation targeting the firm's networks in China. Investigations revealed that the perpetrators behind this incident, apparently based in China, sought both the firm's proprietary information and access to the email accounts used by Chinese human rights activists." [13]

---

12. Gerard Alexander, American Enterprise Institute for Public Policy Research, "Illiberal Europe (*http://www.aei.org/doclib/20060623_otialexanderforposting_g.pdf*)," 2006, page 4

Certainly, many countries engage and enforce online censorship and restrictions on free speech. At the same time, the U.N. is "calling for governments of the world to protect citizens' access to the internet as a key tool for enabling their human rights."[14] One of the requirements for this? Taking meaningful steps to ensure the privacy of personal data.

In keeping with the European privacy view, a new right is being proposed: the right to be forgotten. This proposal would force "companies holding data to allow users to withdraw it from websites."[15] For example, a user could request that Google remove from its search results a newspaper article that harmed their public reputation. Google has already refused a request from Spain to remove search results for an article that criticizes a Spanish plastic surgeon, arguing that this is censorship. Imagine what the Internet would look like if we were all allowed to remove items that don't feature us in a complimentary light.

Issues of privacy are often weighed against other values: free speech, free press, free Internet, safety, and security. Depending on what you hold dear will determine what you will fight to keep and what you will be willing to give up.

Networked Privacy: The "I" Versus the Collective "We"

In a talk at the Personal Democracy Forum 2011, Danah Boyd posited that since our data and interactions are connected, our privacy is connected as well. As a result, privacy is not just about an individual's expectation but involves a network of individuals' expectations, or the collective. Boyd points out:

> "Our laws are focused on data collection, not the usage of data. And, yet, it's at the usage level where the violations of collective privacy take place. It's not particularly creepy to know that someone is a Yankees fan if they're wearing a Yankees T-Shirt. But if your algorithm pieces together thousands of pieces of data shared by that person and their friends and develops a portrait of that person from which to judge them... that's creepy."[16]

Paradoxically, advanced technology has bought us closer to the beginnings of human society—where small groups of hunters and gatherers had a communal living style that precluded any concept of privacy. The digital age has reinvigorated that ancient model

13. 2010 Report to Congress on the U.S.-China Economic and Security Review Commission, "Chapter 5: China and the Internet (*http://www.uscc.gov/annual_report/2010/chapter5_section_1%28page221%29.pdf*)," page 230

14. Aaron Saenz, Singularity Hub, "UN Declares Internet Access A Human Right (*http://singularityhub.com/2011/06/12/un-declares-internet-access-a-human-right-but-fast-and-cheap-may-be-as-important-as-open/*), But Fast and Cheap May Be as Important as Open," June 12, 2011

15. Eva Dou, Reuters, "Internet privacy and the right to be forgotten (*http://www.reuters.com/article/2011/03/17/us-eu-internet-privacy-idustre72g48z20110317*)," March 17, 2011

16. Danah Boyd, Personal Democracy Forum 2011, "Networked Privacy (*http://www.danah.org/papers/talks/2011/pdf2011.html*)," June 6, 2011

of human interaction on a global scale. It is now possible for someone in China to know exactly where and how I live in California, including the height and age of my children and spouse. This is not a new level of intimacy. However, before the digital age that level of intimacy required us to live in the same place, sharing bonds of blood and community that often spanned many generations. Such ties are no longer prerequisites for intimate knowledge of another person's life and the impact of this on individuals and human society in general, no one can predict.

Some of us might argue that privacy no longer exists, others, that no matter where we live, technology advances have always pushed us to revisit and redefine privacy. But while privacy may indeed be networked, it is up to all of us, as individuals and collectives, to help determine what privacy means in the digital age.

Bibliography

1. Professor John Blackie, "The Doctrinal History of Privacy Protection in Unity and Complexity," University of Strathclyde

2. Gerard Alexander, "Illiberal Europe (*http://www.aei.org/doclib/20060623_otialex anderforposting_g.pdf*)," American Institute for Public Policy Research, 2006

3. Jacob Mchangama, National Review Online, "Censorship as Tolerance (*http://www.nationalreview.com/articles/243451/censorship-tolerance-jacob-mchangama*)," July 19, 2010

4. Lauren Effron, ABC NightLine, "Facebook in Your Face: New Facial Recognition Feature Raises a Few Eyebrows (*http://abcnews.go.com/technology/facebook-facial-recognition-feature-raises-eyebrows/story?id=13792666*)," June 10, 2011

5. Wikipedia, "Common Law (*http://en.wikipedia.org/wiki/common_law*)"

6. ushistory.org, Historic Documents, "Bill of Rights and Later Amendments (*http://www.ushistory.org/documents/amendments.htm*)"

7. DeCew, Judity, "Privacy (*http://plato.stanford.edu/archives/fall2008/entries/privacy/*)," The Stanford Encyclopedia of Philosophy (Fall 2008 Edition), Edward N. Zalta (ed.)

8. Warren and Brandeis, Harvard Law Review, "The Right to Privacy (*http://groups.csail.mit.edu/mac/classes/6.805/articles/privacy/privacy_brand_warr2.html*)," Vol. IV, December 15, 1890, No. 5

9. William L. Prosser, California Law Review, "Privacy," Volume 48, Number 3, August 1960, pg. 389

10. Council of Europe, "The European Convention on Human Rights and its Five Protocols," November 4, 1950, Section 1, Article 8

11. Wikipedia, "Law of Obligations (*http://en.wikipedia.org/wiki/law_of_obligations*)"

12. "The Constitution of the United States (*http://www.usconstitution.net/cite.html*)," Amendment 1.

13. Wikipedia, "Free Market (*http://en.wikipedia.org/wiki/free_market*)"

14. Wikipedia, "European Convention on Human Rights (*http://en.wikipedia.org/wiki/european_convention_on_human_rights*)"

15. Wikipedia, "Law of Obligations (*http://en.wikipedia.org/wiki/law_of_obligations*)"

16. Professor Ruth Walden, "Insult Laws: An Insult to Press Freedom (*http://www.wpfc.org/site/docs/pdf/insult%20laws-text.pdf*)," University of North Carolina, Published by the World Press Freedom Committee Rex Rand Fund, 2000

17. The Legal Project, "European Hate Speech Laws (*http://www.legal-project.org/issues/european-hate-speech-laws*)"

18. James Q. Whitman, Ford Foundation Professor of Comparative and Foreign Law, Yale University, "The Two Western Cultures of Privacy: Dignity Versus Liberty (*http://www.yalelawjournal.org/pdf/113-6/whitmanfinal.pdf*)," April 1, 2004

19. Scott Sayare, Maia De La Baume, and Robert Mackey, New York Times, "French Shocked by I.M.F. Chief's Perp Walk (*http://thelede.blogs.nytimes.com/2011/05/16/french-shocked-by-i-m-f-chiefs-perp-walk/*)," May 16, 2011

20. Matt Clarke, Prison Legal News, "Celebrity Justice: Prison Lifestyles of the Rich and Famous (*https://www.prisonlegalnews.org/(x(1)s(je3ujg45tvrextrxtwqyxpzi))/displayarticle.aspx?articleid=22532&aspxautodetectcookiesupport=1*)," August 23, 2011

21. U.S. Department of Health & Human Services, "Understanding Health Information Privacy (*http://www.hhs.gov/ocr/privacy/hipaa/understanding/index.html*)"

22. United Nations, The Universal Declaration of Human Rights (*http://www.un.org/en/documents/udhr/*), Article 12, December 10, 1948

23. McKinsey Global Institute, "Big data: The next frontier for innovation, competition, and productivity (*http://www.mckinsey.com/mgi/publications/big_data/pdfs/mgi_big_data_full_report.pdf*)," June 2011, pg. 19

24. Amar Toor, Aol Tech, "Microsoft's Patriot Act admission has the EU up in arms (*http://www.engadget.com/2011/07/06/microsofts-patriot-act-admission-has-the-eu-up-in-arms/*)," July 6, 2011

25. 2010 Report to Congress on the U.S.-China Economic and Security Review Commission, "Chapter 5: China and the Internet (*http://www.uscc.gov/annual_report/2010/chapter5_section_1%28page221%29.pdf*)," page 230

26. Aaron Saenz, Singularity Hub, "UN Declares Internet Access A Human Right (*http://singularityhub.com/2011/06/12/un-declares-internet-access-a-human-right-but-fast-and-cheap-may-be-as-important-as-open/*), But Fast and Cheap May Be as Important as Open," June 12, 2011

27. Eva Dou, Reuters, "Internet privacy and the right to be forgotten (*http://www.reuters.com/article/2011/03/17/us-eu-internet-privacy-idustre72g48z20110317*)," March 17, 2011

28. Danah Boyd, Personal Democracy Forum 2011, "Networked Privacy (*http://www.danah.org/papers/talks/2011/pdf2011.html*)," June 6, 2011

CHAPTER 3

The Regulators

The Internet has no geographic boundaries. For the most part, its data flows freely. However, just because there are no are no boundaries, it does not necessarily follow that all countries allow the data to flow unchecked. For example, several countries block access to YouTube. China, known for having the most advanced and extensive filtering systems, blocks access to any site that contains keywords, such as "democracy" and "human rights."[1] There is an increasingly alarming trend towards just-in-time Internet blocking where users are prevented access to information at key political inflection points, such as elections or times of social unrest, where the websites of opposition parties, the media, Twitter, and Facebook are blocked as illustrated by the recent Middle East and North African protests. Sometime Internet access is blocked completely, as demonstrated in Egypt where the government was able bring the Internet and cell phone service down.

While the Internet is global, the way we govern and do business is not. We operate as countries or regions and our businesses may be limited to one city or town or may reach around the globe. What one country or region enacts in "the name of privacy," is felt around the world. So, how do countries regulate the collection, use, and protection of their citizen's personal information?

If you live in the U.S., you might argue that very little regulation is going on, pointing to RapLeaf's (*http://online.wsj.com/article/ sb10001424052702304410504575560243259416072.html?mod=djemalertnews*) questionable use of data mining, web scraping, and cookie tracking to build extensive and intrusive dossiers (names included) as well as Apple's caching of location data (*http://arstechnica.com/apple/news/2011/04/how-apple-tracks-your-location-without -your-consent-and-why-it-matters.ars*) via the iPhone and Google's violation of user privacy (*http://www.huffingtonpost.com/2011/03/30/googles-ftc-privacy-settlement -buzz_n_842490.html*) when it launched Google Buzz in 2010. If you live in Europe, you might point to these same incidents as examples of how little regard the U.S. has

---

1. Frank La Rue, United Nations Human Rights Council, "Report of the Special Rapporteur on the promotion and protection of the right to freedom of opinion and expression, May 16,2011, pg. 9

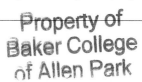

for its citizens' privacy. Both points of view have merit, but perhaps it's less about where one falls on the regulation scale and more about the intrinsic value of privacy:

- Is privacy a commodity that each individual, based on his or her preferences, can sell or rent in return for a service or product?
- Is privacy a basic human right that transcends commoditization, which must be protected at all costs?

Nations, like individuals, have different views on privacy. Certainly, the U.S. seems to regard one's personal information as a commodity and it appears that the European Union (EU) regards privacy as an inalienable right. Of course, culture, politics, and history also play a role. The EU's perceptions of privacy are heavily influenced by history—for example, the Nazis used personal information "collections" to identify, round up, and dispose of "undesirables." One can understand how something so evil can have a tremendous impact on the enactment of laws that protect citizens' personal privacy. In contrast, China's privacy rights (*http://www.economist.com/node/5389362 ?story_id=5389362*), or rather lack of them, is well know and well documented.

What happens when nations' views and expectations of privacy collide? Conflict comes into play as well as spillover (for example, the EU has comprehensive privacy laws but its members can also invoke more aggressive ones). Although the Internet has no boundaries, it is safe to say that every country believes it is their duty to protect their citizens from harm, digital or otherwise.

For companies, meeting or exceeding the myriad of online privacy regulations is a requirement of "doing business." If they don't, access to data (and the consumers who generate most of it) from a specific country or region may be restricted or even cut off. For consumers, privacy policies and expectations range from restrictive to "anything goes." It is left up to them to figure out how to navigate turbulent digital waters. Confusing? Yes, and likely to stay that way for the foreseeable future (sorry, but we believe in calling it like we see it). That being said, before we can look at the current state of privacy regulations, we must first understand the role that government and regulatory agencies play in defining and enforcing privacy policy.

Depending on your citizenship, you may believe that your country is an "enlightened" privacy protector but think again: government surveillance, censorship, and the collection and monitoring of personal information is on the rise worldwide. Suffice to say, while much of the privacy debate is focused on protecting the individual from intrusive advertising and keeping sensitive healthcare, financial, and religious information private, our "protectors" are directly responsible for significant privacy erosions. While most governments believe their citizen's privacy needs to be protected from the commercial sector, they don't apply the same logic to themselves.

A (Very) Brief History of "Digital" Privacy Regulation

However you look at it, the concept of the "right to privacy" has been around since human kind began. Certainly, legal protections can be traced back to the Greek and Roman civilizations and in Western countries for hundreds of years. (For a complete look at the evolution of our right to privacy, see Chapter 2.) In the 1970's, we begin to see privacy combined with the concept of data protection (in keeping with the rise of the Internet as discussed in Chapter 1). The first data protection law was enacted in the Land of Hesse in Germany (1970), followed by national laws in Sweden (1973), the U.S. (1974), Germany (1977), and France (1978).

In the 1980's, comprehensive privacy guidelines were developed to keep pace with the ongoing digital explosion. For example, The Council of Europe's 1981 Convention for the Protection of Individuals with regard to the Automatic Process of Personal Data (*http://conventions.coe.int/treaty/en/treaties/html/108.htm*) (Strasbourg, 1981) and OECD (Organization for Economic Co-operation and Development) Guidelines Governing the Protection of Privacy and Transborder Data Flows of Personal Data (*http:// www.oecd.org/document/18/0,3746,en_2649_34255_1815186_1_1_1_1,00&&en-uss _01dbc.html*) (1980) set out specific rules about the collection, storage, and dissemination of personal information. (OECD members include: Austria, Canada, Denmark, France, Germany, Norway, Sweden, and the U.S.) As digital capacity and capabilities evolved, specific privacy legislation was enacted by a number of countries and regions. Much of that legislation is based on these guidelines.

How is it that these guidelines served to create very different kinds of privacy legislation in terms of scope and impact? Certainly, culture, history, and the notion of privacy itself all play a role in each nation's attempt to define and enforce privacy regulations. But although all countries like to think of themselves as "uniquely formed," every country's privacy regulatory activities have certain attributes and can be categorized into four groups.

Privacy Regulatory Models—Complimentary or Contradictory?

While regulatory models can be categorized, it does not follow that these groups are mutually exclusive. In other words, parts of each group can be "adopted" simultaneously which some may call complimentary and others may call contradictory. For readers like ourselves that fall under the U.S. regulatory model, we would wager that contradictory would be the nicest word used to describe it. In any case, here are the models:

- **Comprehensive laws (or regulatory model).** In this case, general laws govern the collection and use of personal information by public and private sectors and these laws are typically accompanied by an oversight body (with or without real teeth) to ensure compliance. The EU is considered the canonical example of this model. Canada and Australia use a variant of this, a co-regulatory model where the data collection industries develop the privacy protection rules and those rules are enforced by industry and overseen by a privacy agency. On the scale of privacy viewed as a commodity or privacy viewed as a fundamental civic right, countries that enact comprehensive privacy laws are usually far more civically inclined.

- **Sectoral laws (targeted model)**. In this model, countries favor specific sectoral laws that govern specific items, like video rental records or financial privacy, where enforcement is achieved through a range of mechanisms (like regulatory agencies, federal and state statutes, and self-policing). This means that new legislation is introduced whenever new technology raises privacy concerns. In many countries, sectoral laws are combined with general legislation that targets specific categories of information, like telecommunications, police files, or credit records. In countries where intellectual property is a major economic driver, this model often leads to conflict between technology vendors and large intellectual property (IP) holders. (IP holders fear that the combination of new digital technologies and anonymity aids IP piracy—this is discussed in Chapter 4). And yes, this forms the basis of the very complicated U.S. privacy regulatory model.

- **Self-regulation**. In this model, various forms of self-regulation are employed. As a result companies and industry bodies are expected to establish codes of practice and engage in self-policing. For example, in the U.S. companies like TRUSTe (*http://learn.truste.com/content/search_amer_privacy_brand_learnmoreq211?campaign =70180000000tc5k&campaign_theme=privacy&campaign_tactic=keyword_amer _privacy_google_brand_exact_learnmore&leadsource_detail=keyword_amer_pri vacy_google_brand_exact_learnmore&le*), Verisign (*http://www.verisign.com/*), and BBBOnLine (*http://www.bbb.org/us/bbb-online-business/*) offer businesses a way to certify that they meet the "highest standards of online privacy." The clear conflict of interest in this model disturbs many privacy advocates. For example, in the U.S. privacy and security disputes often end up in civil court.

- **Consumer regulation**. In this model, privacy protection is employed by the consumer through the use of commercial digital privacy protection tools (*http://epic .org/privacy/tools.html*). There are now a wide number of programs and systems available that provide varying degrees of privacy and security. They include anonymous remailers and proxies, cookie blockers, encryptors for the secure transmission of email, IMs, files, and even voice, and alternate networks. Keep in mind that these tools may not effectively protect privacy and that some of them were primarily designed to help law enforcement access your "personal information." The number and scope of privacy tools, systems, and software, companies that may change the privacy landscape, as well as how these very same items can be used against you by individuals or government agencies, are covered in Chapter 4.

It is safe to say that every country, or federation of countries, employs attributes from some, or all, of these models to drive privacy policy and regulations. However, there is a continuum that holds equally true: countries either regulate from a comprehensive, all-encompassing view (where privacy policy is pushed down and out) or from a more segmented approach (where policy is targeted at a specific sector and employs a number of different ways to drive it—in other words, policy is only driven up when forced by the citizenry). The EU and U.S. are excellent examples of these two extremes.

The U.S. Regulatory Model—A Bottom Up Approach

While the U.S. may not have a comprehensive digital privacy law, there are two industries and one population segment that, from a privacy standpoint, are heavily regulated via federal laws:

- **Health care industry**. The Health Information and Portability Accountability Act (*http://www.hhs.gov/ocr/privacy/hipaa/understanding/index.html*) (HIPAA) protects private health information held by "covered entities" (like health care providers, insurance carriers, company health plans, and any organization that processes health information). There are a number of administrative, physical, and technical safeguards used to assure the confidentiality, integrity, and availability of electronic protected health information. The Privacy Rule gives the consumer rights over their health information and sets rules on who can access and receive health information.

- **Financial industry**. The Gramm-Leach-Bliley (GLB) Act (*http://business.ftc.gov/privacy-and-security/gramm-leach-bliley-act*) requires financial institutions (companies that offer financial products or services like credit cards, loans, or advice) to explain how it collects, shares, and protects customers' data via a privacy notice that is annually updated. It includes a Safeguards Rule (*http://en.wikipedia.org/wiki/gramm%e2%80%93leach%e2%80%93bliley_act*) that requires companies to develop and enforce a written information security and pretexting protection that prevents unauthorized access to "personal nonpublic" information.

- **Children under the age of 13**. The Children's Online Privacy Protection Act (*http://www.coppa.org/comply.htm*) (COPPA) requires all websites that collect information from children under the age of 13 to have an explicit privacy policy, delineates the website owner's responsibilities to protect children's online privacy and safety, as well as the conditions under which the owner must receive verifiable consent from a parent.

In addition to these key areas, there are over a hundred federal and state statutes that define and regulate some area of privacy. For example, "forty-six states, the District of Columbia, Puerto Rico, and the Virgin Islands (*http://www.aicpa.org/interestareas/informationtechnology/resources/privacy/federalstateandotherprofessionalregulations/stateprivacyregulations/pages/default.aspx*) have enacted privacy regulations requiring companies and/or state agencies disclose to consumers security breaches involving personal information,"[2] four states (*http://www.ncsl.org/default.aspx?tabid=13463*) have laws related to the privacy policies for web sites, and sixteen states have laws related to the privacy policies for government web sites and state portals. Added to that, there are a number of regulatory agencies that engage in reactive monitoring and enforcement penalties (yes, it is that complicated and no, it's not going to get better any time soon).

The Federal Trade Commission (FTC)

Created in 1914, the FTC's purpose was to "bust the trusts (*http://www.ftc.gov/ftc/about.shtm*)" and over the years it has gained broader authority with enforcement and administrative responsibilities under more than 70 laws (GLB and COPPA included), especially in the area of consumer protection laws which includes the Fair Credit Reporting Act (*http://en.wikipedia.org/wiki/fair_credit_reporting_act*) (FCRA, 1970), the Telemarketing Sales Rule (*http://ecfr.gpoaccess.gov/cgi/t/text/text-idx?c=ecfr&sid=af82ca9f5358ec851e8d272cae1627d4&rgn=div5&view=text&node=16:1.0.1.3.34&idno=16#16:1.0.1.3.34.0.32.1*), the Pay-Per-Call Rule, and the Equal Opportunity Credit Act (*http://www.ftc.gov/bcp/edu/pubs/consumer/credit/cre15.shtm*). It is fair to say that the FTC is the clearing center for most digital privacy issues and certainly takes the lead on digital privacy, most recently proposing a "normative framework for how companies should protect consumers' privacy off- and on-line."

The FTC employs two different models to protect consumer's personal information:

- **Notice and Choice**. This model encourages companies to develop privacy notices (the ubiquitous privacy policy which describes how personal information is collected and used so that the consumer can decide for themselves). Today, almost every website has a privacy policy which is probably too long and incomprehensible. In fact, a recent Carnegie Mellon University (*http://arstechnica.com/tech-pol icy/news/2008/10/study-reading-online-privacy-policies-could-cost-365-billion-a -year.ars*) study points out that if Americans actually read the privacy policies for the major sites they encountered, they would spend on average 200 hours per person, per year.

- **Harm-Based**. This model focuses on protecting consumers from specific harms (like their physical security, economic injury, or unwanted intrusions into daily lives). As current litigation efforts (*http://www.privacysecuritysource.com/under standing-proposed-models-for-privacy/*) show, the ability to prove "harm" and show "actual damage" is often difficult, which results in lengthy and costly court

---

2. American Institute of CPAs, "State Privacy Regulations (*http://www.aicpa.org/interestareas/ informationtechnology/resources/privacy/federalstateandotherprofessionalregulations/ stateprivacyregulations/pages/default.aspx*)"

cases. At the same time, this model is "after the fact" and offers companies no proactive guidance on how to protect private information.

The FTC is trying to address the shortcomings in both models, proposing a Framework (*http://www.ftc.gov/opa/2010/12/privacyreport.shtm*) that companies should follow to protect consumers' privacy and that policymakers should consider as they develop solutions, policies, and laws based on the concept of Privacy by Design (*http://www.ipc.on.ca/english/privacy/introduction-to-pbd/*) (PbD).

The Federal Communications Commission (FCC)

Established in 1934 by the Communications Act, the FCC (*http://www.fcc.gov/what-we-do*) regulates interstate and international communications by radio, television, wire, satellite, and cable in all states, the District of Columbia and U.S. territories. While the FCC is not likely to take the lead on privacy issues, it does address those privacy matters that touch on FCC regulated areas such as common carriers, cable carriers, and telemarketing. The FCC is currently working with the FTC to define its role in privacy issues (surrounding location based services and mobile applications (*http://www.adlawaccess.com/2011/05/articles/privacy-and-information-securi/fcc-announces-june-28-2011-location-based-service-lbs-forum/*)) and is taking the lead on the development of a Cybersecurity Roadmap (*http://www.utcinsight.org/content/fcc-working-cybersecurity-roadmap-communications-networks-seeks-comments*) which identifies the five most critical cybersecurity threats (such as malicious traffic and other security vulnerabilities) to the communications infrastructure (public Internet) and its end-users and develops a two-year plan to mitigate them.

The Department of Commerce (Commerce)

Originally created as the United States Department of Commerce and Labor in 1903, Commerce (*http://en.wikipedia.org/wiki/united_states_department_of_commerce*) is a Cabinet department of the U.S. government that is focused on promoting economic growth. It is primarily engaged in gathering economic and demographic data for business and government decision-making, issuing patents and trademarks, and setting industrial standards. Not to be confused with the FTC's Privacy Framework, Commerce released its own privacy report (*http://www.commerce.gov/node/12471*), entitled "Commercial Data Privacy and Innovation in the Internet Economy: A Dynamic Policy Framework." This Framework is "designed to protect privacy, transparency, and informed choice while also recognizing the importance of improving customer service, recognizing the dynamic nature of both technologies and markets and encouraging continued innovation over time." Its recommendations include: the reinstitution of Fair Market Information Practice Principles (a sort of online Privacy Bill of Rights), the standardization of industry privacy policies, the establishment of a Privacy Policy Office that works directly with the FTC, actively reaching out to trading partners to "bridge differences in privacy frameworks," streamlining the various state-level data security breach notification levels, etc.

The Department of Energy (DOE)

Formed in 1977, the DOE (*http://www.energy.gov/about/index.htm*) is a Cabinet-level department of the U.S. government. It assumed the responsibilities of the Federal Energy Administration, the Energy Research and Development Administration, the Federal Power Commission, and several other various agency programs. Its main focus is to address energy, environmental, and nuclear challenges while ensuring U.S. security. As it works on modernizing the electrical grid through the promotion of Smart Grid technologies (*http://www.energy.gov/news/9644.htm*) (which produce detailed energy-usage data), it is also developing policies to protect consumer privacy and choice. For example: allowing the consumer to opt in to "trusted" third party use of energy-usage data.

The Department of Health and Human Services (HHS)

The HHS (*http://www.hhs.gov/about/*) is a Cabinet-level department of the U.S. government. It is tasked with protecting the health of all Americans and providing essential human resources. The HHS represents almost "a quarter of all federal outlays" while administering "more grant dollars than all other federal agencies combined." While the FTC has administrative and enforcement responsibilities for most privacy regulations, the HHS is responsible for enforcing the HIPAA Privacy Rule and is known for assessing hefty civil penalties (*http://www.hhs.gov/ocr/privacy/hipaa/news/cignetnews.html*) for violations.

The Consumer Financial Protection Bureau (CFPB)

The CFPB (*http://www.consumerfinance.gov/*) was established by the Dodd-Frank Wall Street Reform and Consumer Protection Act of 2010 (*http://thomas.loc.gov/cgi-bin/query/z?c111:h.r.4173:*). It is an independent bureau established within the Federal Reserve System and its mission is to help consumers make "financial decisions that are best for them and their families (*http://www.treasury.gov/initiatives/pages/cfpb.aspx*)." The CFPB will take the lead on financial product and services protection while the FTC retains enforcement authority and takes the lead on data security. Currently undergoing heavy resistance by the bank lobby, the financial services industry, and the GOP (*http://www.thenation.com/article/161069/bank-lobby-steps-its-attack-elizabeth-warren*), it is not clear how much "real" authority the CFPB will have.

Some Final Words on the U.S. Model

While it is absolutely true that the U.S. privacy regulatory model is complicated and departmentalized, it does not follow that the U.S. has little or no privacy regulations or guidelines (as you've seen in this section, there are actually quite a lot!). In certain areas, like HIPAA, the U.S. has provided comprehensive guidelines and enforcement teeth. But the U.S. model of privacy is based on privacy as a commodity, leaving it up to the consumer (whether we like it or not) to remain vigilant about privacy matters and to call for more regulation in certain areas as problems arise. As a result, we have lots of federal and state privacy laws, numerous regulatory agencies, and of course, the judicial system weighing in. That being said, the two Frameworks pushed by the FTC and Commerce are certainly an indication that the U.S. is taking a more proactive approach to privacy, focusing on comprehensive guidelines that businesses and consumers can understand.

The European Union Model—A Top Down Approach

The EU is considered to be a trailblazer in enacting rigorous privacy protection policies and laws that favor the individual. The right to privacy is in the constitutions of many EU countries, such as Germany and Spain. But keep in mind that while the U.S. privacy laws are piecemeal, its modern concept of the right to privacy can be found in several amendments in the Bill of Rights, held by the Supreme Court as penumbral rights of privacy (*http://plato.stanford.edu/entries/privacy/*). (We cover all of this in Chapter 2.)

Europe's explicit support of a right to privacy can be found in the European Convention on Human Rights (*http://en.wikipedia.org/wiki/european_convention_on_human_rights*) (ECHR), an international treaty designed to protect human rights in Europe. Ratified in 1953, the ECHR was a way to codify and strengthen "the protection of fundamental rights in the light of changes and technological developments."[3] (All EU member states are also signatories on the ECHR.) In Section 1, Article 8, the right to privacy is recognized: "Everyone has the right (*http://www.hri.org/docs/echr50.html#c.seci*) to respect for his private and family life, his home, and his correspondence." Certainly, the seeds for the EU's comprehensive privacy policy can be traced back to the ECHR.

Prior to 1995, however, privacy laws varied widely across Europe. The OECD (1980) guidelines regarding the protection of privacy as it applied to "data flows," were nonbinding (and no one fully implemented them). However, in 1995 the EU enacted the Data Protection Directive (*http://en.wikipedia.org/wiki/data_protection_directive*) which incorporated the OECD's eight principles (we are paraphrasing here so for the full text, go to the actual source (*http://www.oecd.org/document/18/0,3746,en_2649_34255_1815186_1_1_1_1,00.html*)[4]) for the protection of personal data:

3. Lauren Movius & Nathalie Krup, International Journal of Communica9780735662100tion 3 (2009), 169-187, "U.S. and EU Privacy Policy: Comparison of Regulatory Approaches," pg. 4

4. URL: *http://www.oecd.org/document/18/0,3746,en_2649_34255_1815186_1_1_1_1,00.html*

- **Collection Limitation**. There should be limits to the collection of personal data, it should be lawfully collected, with the knowledge or consent of the individual who "owns" the data.
- **Data Quality**. Personal data should only be used for its stated purpose and should be accurate, complete, and up-to-date.
- **Purpose Specification**. The purpose(s) for the data collected should be clearly specified and the data subject must be notified each time the purpose is changed.
- **Use Limitation**. Personal data cannot be disclosed or used differently than specified unless the data subject consents or by authority of law.
- **Security Safeguards**. Personal data should be kept secure from potential abuse.
- **Openness**. Data collectors should be transparent on how personal data is collected, used, and shared.
- **Individual Participation**. Data subjects should be informed about who is collecting and using their data and have access to that data to make corrections.
- **Accountability**. Data collectors must be held accountable for creating a system that complies with these principles.

The Directive, made up of thirty-three articles in eight chapters, was designed to provide a regulatory framework for the "secure and free (*http://epic.org/privacy/intl/eu_data _protection_directive.html*) movement of personal data across the national borders of the EU member countries, in addition to setting a baseline of security around personal information wherever it is stored, transmitted or processed."[5]

In the Directive (as in the OECD guidelines), data subjects have explicit rights and each EU country's data protection commissioner or agency enforces those rights. Additionally, all countries that do business with the EU are expected to abide by these rules.

Over the years, in keeping with technology advances, other directives have been added. The Telecommunication Privacy Directive (1997 (*http://www.oceg.org/view/15556*)) specifically addressed the obligations that carriers and service providers had to protect the privacy of citizen's communications, including Internet-related activities. In 2002, the Privacy and Communications Directive (*http://eur-lex.europa.eu/lexuriserv/lexuri serv.do?uri=oj:l:2002:201:0037:0047:en:pdf*), addressed new digital technologies in the treatment of private information as it relates to traffic data, spam, and cookies. It addresses (*http://en.wikipedia.org/wiki/directive_on_privacy_and_electronic_communi cations*) both data security, requiring providers to deliver a secure environment and notify subscribers of breaches, as well as the level of confidentiality that is expected (for example, no listening, tapping, or storage of information unless explicit consent is given). The directive also includes a data retention policy where the provider must erase or anonymize data when it is no longer needed. However, the directive also gave mem-

5. Electronic Privacy Information Center, "EU Data Protection Directive (*http://epic.org/privacy/intl/eu_data _protection_directive.html*)"

ber states permission to amend the policy, determining on a country-by-country basis due to the needs of public and state security, defense, and law.

In 2006, the EU enacted the Data Retention Directive (*http://eur-lex.europa.eu/lexuri serv/lexuriserv.do?uri=oj:l:2006:105:0054:0063:en:pdf*), which attempted to "harmonize the member states' provisions relating to the retention of communications data (*http://www.theregister.co.uk/2006/02/24/data_retention_directive_ratified/*)"[6] and was considered by many to be a serious erosion of privacy protections for citizens. The directive, created after the terrorist attacks in London and Madrid, mandated a six month (*http://www.dw-world.de/dw/article/0,,15120172,00.html*) (and up to two years) storage of all telecom and Internet data to aid law enforcement anti-terrorist activities. Met with outrage (*http://www.eff.org/deeplinks/2010/03/beginning-end-data-retention*) by European citizens (the Freedom Not Fear mass protests across Europe) member state laws that complied with the directive in Romania and Germany have been struck down as a violation of human rights which has set the stage for upcoming suits in other member countries. Currently, the EU is proposing an update (*http://epic.org/privacy/ intl/eu_data_protection_directive.html*) to the directive that strengthens the rights of individuals and extends those protections to the police and criminal systems.

The Safe Harbor Effect

The EU's Data Protection Directive applied to member and non-member countries. In other words, if non-member countries wanted to do business with the EU they had to comply with the directive. But the U.S.'s approach of segmented federal and state privacy legislation, regulation, and industry self-regulation is very different from the EU's comprehensive approach. In order to ensure that business continued between the U.S. and EU member countries, the U.S. Department of Commerce and the FTC, working with the EU, adopted a Safe Harbor Framework that would allow U.S. companies to transfer, store, or use personal information about EU member country residents if they met the "adequacy standard" of the Data Protection Directive.

The Safe Harbor agreement allowed U.S. corporations to certify to Commerce that they had joined a self-regulatory organization that adhered to the seven Safe Harbor Principles (similar to those laid out in the OECD **guidelines**) or had implemented a privacy policy that conformed to those principles. In others words, a company can indicate that they conform to the principles in a stated privacy policy or join a self-regulatory privacy program (*http://itlaw.wikia.com/wiki/safe_harbor_agreement*) that adheres to those principles (for example, TRUSTe's EU Safe Harbor Seal Program (*http://www .truste.com/privacy_seals_and_services/enterprise_privacy/eu_safe_harbor_seal.html*)). In keeping with the U.S.'s current regulatory environment, enforcement is accomplished via the FTC, other U.S. agencies, and federal and state laws.

---

6. The Register, "Data Retention Directive receives rubber stamp (*http://www.theregister.co.uk/2006/02/24/ data_retention_directive_ratified/*)," February 24, 2006

Some Final Words on the EU Model

Informed by history, as illustrated by the use of private information against its own citizens in World War II as well as the rise of communism in the 1950s, the EU views privacy as a basic human right that must be rigorously defended. The EU's successful comprehensive legislation and enforcement of privacy laws makes the case for the standardization of global privacy policies and laws that all countries could adopt. Even for countries that have a more sectoral approach to privacy, this would be simpler as it would mean the development and enforcement of only one "Safe Harbor-like" agreement. However, keep in mind that the EU, like the U.S., has certainly relaxed its stance on privacy when balanced with issues of security since the events of September 11, 2001. The constant and often violent tug of war between individual privacy and national security is a common theme across the globe.

A Quick Tour of Other Country's Privacy Laws

Although we do not intend this chapter to be an extensive (and exhaustive) drill-down on each country's privacy laws, we will say this: nearly every country in the world recognizes a right to privacy, either in their Constitutions (*http://gilc.org/privacy/survey/ intro.html*), through the courts, or through the adoption of international agreements (like the ECHR). For example, like the EU, Australia and Canada have comprehensive laws. There are also other regional privacy initiatives, like the Asia-Pacific Economic Cooperation (APEC) initiative. APEC, made up of 21 member countries in the Asia Pacific region, released its Privacy Framework in 2004. It was met with some controversy—critics on one side arguing that the Framework was far weaker than the OECD and EU approach while others saw it as a way to develop higher privacy standards in Asia. But APEC persevered and in 2010 announced (*http://www.apec.org/en/press/news -releases/2010/0716_ecsg_cpea.aspx*) a new Cross-border Privacy Enforcement Arrangement (CPEA) designed to facilitate "information sharing and cooperation between authorities responsible for data and consumer protection in the APEC region." This new arrangement works with regional privacy regulatory legislation that is already in place, like the EU's, and is certainly a sign that the globalization of privacy laws and policies is a possibility.

No overview of privacy would be complete without a discussion of China. If the U.S. is an example of the commoditization of privacy and the EU is an example of privacy as an inalienable human right, than China would probably best be characterized as a nation with no regard for its citizens' privacy or anyone else's. There are numerous examples of its monitoring and surveillance capabilities. It monitors all "Skype traffic (*http://www.zdnet.com/blog/btl/the-cost-of-doing-business-in-china-privacy/10277*) for keywords that may offend the Communist party."[7] It asked for and received support

---

7. Larry Dignan, ZDNet, "The cost of doing business in China: Privacy (*http://www.zdnet.com/blog/btl/the -cost-of-doing-business-in-china-privacy/10277*)," October 2, 2008

(*http://www.economist.com/node/5389362?story_id=5389362*) from Microsoft to shut down a blog authored by an outspoken critic and Yahoo helped to trace the identity of a Chinese Internet user for revealing secrets. It attempted to hack into Google Gmail accounts of "hundreds of users (*http://www.huffingtonpost.com/2011/06/01/google -gmail-hack-china_n_869995.html*), including senior U.S. government officials, Chinese activists and journalists."[8] Here's Larry Digan's, Editor in Chief of ZDNet and SmartPlanet, take on China and privacy: "China monitors your stuff. China doesn't know the concept of privacy and it isn't likely to care unless its people stand up and revolt–and they aren't."[9] We could not have said it better ourselves.

For a comprehensive list of international privacy and security breach laws, we direct you to Ariel Silverstone's Security Blog (*http://arielsilverstone.com/resources/interna tional-privacy/*).[10] It includes a breakdown of regional (unions) and country laws and is, we have to say, equally informative and frightening as it includes those countries that do not consider privacy a basic human right.

Privacy Versus Security and Safety

No discussion of privacy and its issues can be had without weighing its virtues against security and safety. In most countries, privacy laws are running behind technology, leaving protection gaps and giving rise to digital intrusions. Additionally, law enforcement and intelligence agencies are given broad powers to conduct digital surveillance regardless of privacy laws.

In the U.S, the PATRIOT Act (*http://en.wikipedia.org/wiki/usa_patriot_act*), passed into law after September 11, broadly expanded government authority by reducing restrictions on law enforcement to search telephone and email communications as well as medical, financial, and other records. It also eased restrictions on foreign intelligence gathering in the U.S., allowed for the monitoring and regulation of financial transactions (especially for those foreign individuals and entities), and made it much easier to deport immigrants suspected of terrorism-related acts. Finally, it expanded the definition of terrorism to include domestic terrorism—meaning that all U.S. citizens could be subject to this type of intelligence gathering.

---

8. Alexei Oreskovic and Edwin Chan, Huffpost Tech, "Google: Gmail Hack Likely From China Cyberattackers (*http://www.huffingtonpost.com/2011/06/01/google-gmail-hack-china_n_869995.html*),"

9. Larry Dignan, ZDNet, "The cost of doing business in China: Privacy (*http://www.zdnet.com/blog/btl/the -cost-of-doing-business-in-china-privacy/10277*)," October 2, 2008

10. URL: *http://arielsilverstone.com/resources/international-privacy/*

Other countries are also shifting away from privacy and towards safety and security. France's 2005 anti-terrorist law (*http://www.forbes.com/feeds/afx/2005/12/22/afx2410169.html*) called for "increase(ed) video surveillance of railways stations, airports and other public areas, permit(ted) official snooping on the internet and mobile telephone records, and lengthen(ed) the period of detention for terrorist suspects."[11] The U.K.'s Prevention of Terrorism Act (*http://www.hrw.org/en/news/2005/03/14/uk-new-terrorism-law-fundamentally-flawed*) (2005) allows for control orders restricting the freedom of terrorism suspects. Control order restrictions include (*http://www.liberty-human-rights.org.uk/policy/reports/prevention-of-terrorism-act-2005-summary.pdf*): placing them under house arrest, controlling access to phones and the Internet, and restricting who they meet or communicate with. Its Counter Terrorism Act of 2008 (*http://www.ehow.com/facts_6770131_counter-terrorism-act-2008.html*) broadens law enforcement powers, creating a registration database of all persons convicted for an act of terror or related offenses, expanding the rights to detain and interrogate suspected terrorists, and providing enhanced evidence collection through the use of electronic surveillance equipment. Canada's Anti-Terrorism Act (*http://en.wikipedia.org/wiki/canadian_anti-terrorism_act*) (2001) allows the police to arrest suspects without a warrant and detain them for three days without charges if they believe a terrorist act may be committed and allows judges to compel witnesses to testify in secret about past associations or pending acts under penalty of jail.

According to the U.S. State Department's most recent annual report on Human Rights (*http://www.nytimes.com/2011/04/09/world/middleeast/09rights.html*), more than "40 countries restrict online access to varying degrees, while more than 90 countries have laws controlling organizations."[12] This includes the illegal monitoring of the communications of political opponents, human rights workers, journalists, and labor organizers.

Data Never Dies

One of the reasons Europe has a more comprehensive approach to privacy grows out of its own history where government data was extensively used to target, often fatally, political opponents, minorities and others during World War II and the Cold War. By and large, the data that was misused was collected by governments that were considered relatively benign before they fell from power. This is a perfect example of why regulations or any legal construct should not be confused with things that are truly constant. Digital data does not care how or by whom it is used. It is inevitable that governments change, laws change, social mores change; but data once collected and placed on a global distributed network, such as the Internet, is for all practical purposes, immortal.

---

11. AFX News Limited, Forbes, "French parliament adopts tough anti-terrorism law (*http://www.forbes.com/feeds/afx/2005/12/22/afx2410169.html*)," December 12, 2005

12. Steven Lee Meyers, New York Times, "Rights Abuses Extend Across Middle East, Report Says (*http://www.nytimes.com/2011/04/09/world/middleeast/09rights.html?_r=2*)," April 8, 2011

The laws to regulate how data is used once it is collected are both admirable and necessary. But it is the regulations that *prevent data collection without user consent* that provide the true hope for a reasonable expectation of privacy.

Enlightened or Otherwise, We All Have Skin in This Game

Whatever our respective country's regulatory stance is on a right to privacy, it's clear that our regulators take a different view when it comes to safety and security. In our quest to introduce policy to regulate the commercial aspects of our protection, we may forget that the collection, use, and retention of our personal information represents great value, not only to those who want to steal our information for illegal means, but to our governments for intelligence purposes.

It is safe to say that in the past decade, safety and security concerns have outweighed our right to privacy. Much of the anti-terrorist legislation is in reaction to the September 11 attacks, the Madrid train bombings, the attack on London's transit system, and far too many other attacks in far too many countries (*http://en.wikipedia.org/wiki/list_of _terrorist_incidents*) to enumerate here. The question we should be asking ourselves is this: does our "right to privacy" extend to law enforcement and other government agencies? It is certainly the question that the EU is asking in its updated **Directive** and it is a question that we continue to explore in Chapter 4 as we consider the various players, governments included, who the impact the privacy debate.

Bibliography

1. Frank La Rue, United Nations Human Rights Council, "Report of the Special Rapporteur on the promotion and protection of the right to freedom of opinion and expression, May 16,2011

2. Emily Steel, Wall Street Journal, "A Web Pioneer Profiles Users by Name (*http:// online.wsj.com/article/sb10001424052702304410504575560243259416072.html ?mod=djemalertnews*)," October 25, 2010

3. Jacqui Cheng, ARS Technica, "How Apple tracks your location without consent, and why it matters (*http://arstechnica.com/apple/news/2011/04/how-apple-tracks -your-location-without-your-consent-and-why-it-matters.ars*)," April 20, 2011

4. Bianca Bosker, HuffPost Tech, "Google's FTC Settlement Over Privacy Breach Makes History (*http://www.huffingtonpost.com/2011/03/30/googles-ftc-privacy-set tlement-buzz_n_842490.html*)," March 30, 2011

5. The Economist, "The long march to privacy (*http://www.economist.com/node/ 5389362?story_id=5389362*)," January 12, 2006

6. Jonathan Stempel, Huffpost Tech, "China, Baidu Sued in U.S. For Internet Censorship (*http://www.huffingtonpost.com/2011/05/19/china-baidu-sued-internet-cen sorship_n_864006.html*)," May 19, 2011

7. Meg Roggensack, Huffpost Tech, "Facebook Faces China Censorship Dilemma (*http://www.huffingtonpost.com/human-rights-first/facebook-faces-china-cens_b_852031.html*)," April 21, 2011

8. Council of Europe, "Convention for the Protection of Individuals with regard to Automatic Processing of Personal Data (*http://conventions.coe.int/treaty/en/treaties/html/108.htm*)," January, 28, 1981

9. Directorate for Science, Technology, and Industry, "OECD Guidelines on the Protection of Privacy and Transborder Flows of Personal Data (*http://www.oecd.org/document/18/0,3746,en_2649_34255_1815186_1_1_1_1,00&&en-uss_01dbc.html*)"

10. Electronic Privacy Information Center, "EPIC Online Guide to Practical Privacy Tools (*http://epic.org/privacy/tools.html*)"

11. U.S. Department of Health & Human Services, "Understanding Health Information Privacy (*http://www.hhs.gov/ocr/privacy/hipaa/understanding/index.html*)"

12. Federal Trade Commission, Bureau of Consumer Protection Business Center, "Gramm-Leach-Bliley Act (*http://business.ftc.gov/privacy-and-security/gramm-leach-bliley-act*)"

13. Wikipedia, "Gramm-Leach-Bliley Act (*http://en.wikipedia.org/wiki/gramm%e2%80%93leach%e2%80%93bliley_act*)"

14. COPPA—Children's Online Privacy Protection Act, "How to comply with Children's Online Privacy Protection Act (*http://www.coppa.org/comply.htm*)"

15. AICPA American Institute of CPAs, "State Privacy Regulations (*http://www.aicpa.org/interestareas/informationtechnology/resources/privacy/federalstateandotherprofessionalregulations/stateprivacyregulations/pages/default.aspx*)"

16. National Conference of State Legislatures, "Selected State Laws Related to Internet Privacy (*http://www.ncsl.org/default.aspx?tabid=13463*)"

17. Federal Trade Commission, "About the Federal Trade Commission (*http://www.ftc.gov/ftc/about.shtm*)"

18. Wikipedia, "Fair Credit Reporting Act (*http://en.wikipedia.org/wiki/fair_credit_reporting_act*)"

19. Electronic Code of Federal Regulations, "Telemarketing Sales Rule 16 CFR Part 310 (*http://ecfr.gpoaccess.gov/cgi/t/text/text-idx?c=ecfr&sid=af82ca9f5358ec851e8d272cae1627d4&rgn=div5&view=text&node=16:1.0.1.3.34&idno=16#16:1.0.1.3.34.0.32.1*)"

20. Federal Trade Commission, "Equal Credit Opportunity: Understanding Your Rights Under the Law (*http://www.ftc.gov/bcp/edu/pubs/consumer/credit/cre15.shtm*)"

21. Nate Anderson, ARS Technica, Law & Disorder, "Study: Reading online privacy policies could cost $365 billion a year (*http://www.ftc.gov/bcp/edu/pubs/consumer/credit/cre15.shtm*)," October 8, 2008]

22. Andy Serwin, Privacy & Security Source, "Understanding Proposed Models for Privacy (*http://www.privacysecuritysource.com/understanding-proposed-models-for-privacy/*)," January 15, 2011

23. Federal Trade Commission, "FTC Staff Issues Privacy Report, Offers Framework for Consumers, Businesses, and Policymakers (*http://www.ftc.gov/opa/2010/12/privacyreport.shtm*)," December 1, 2010

24. Information and Privacy Commissioner, Ontario, Canada, "Introduction to PbD (*http://www.ipc.on.ca/english/privacy/introduction-to-pbd/*)"

25. FCC, "What We Do (*http://www.fcc.gov/what-we-do*)"

26. AD Law Access, "FCC Announces June 28, 2011 Location Based Services (LBS) Forum (*http://www.adlawaccess.com/2011/05/articles/privacy-and-information-securi/fcc-announces-june-28-2011-location-based-service-lbs-forum/*)," May 25, 2011

27. Neha Shah, UTC Insight, "FCC Working on Cybersecurity Roadmap for Communications Networks; Seeks Comments (*http://www.utcinsight.org/content/fcc-working-cybersecurity-roadmap-communications-networks-seeks-comments*)," August 9, 2010

28. Wikipedia, "United States Department of Commerce (*http://en.wikipedia.org/wiki/united_states_department_of_commerce*)"

29. U.S. Department of Commerce, "Internet Policy Task Force Privacy Green Paper (*http://www.commerce.gov/node/12471*)"

30. Department of Energy, "About DOE (*http://www.energy.gov/about/index.htm*)"

31. Department of Energy, "New DOE Reports on Smart Grid Technologies Seek to Promote Innovation, Privacy and Access (*http://www.energy.gov/news/9644.htm*)," October 5, 2010

32. U.S. Department of Health & Human Services, "About HHS (*http://www.hhs.gov/about/*)"

33. U.S. Department of Health & Human Services, "HHS Imposes a $4.3 Million Civil Money Penalty for HIPAA Privacy Rule Violations (*http://www.hhs.gov/ocr/privacy/hipaa/news/cignetnews.html*)," February 22, 2011

34. The Consumer Financial Protection Bureau, "Know Before You Owe (*http://www.consumerfinance.gov/knowbeforeyouowe/*)"

35. The Library of Congress, "Wall Street Reform and Consumer Protection Act of 2009 (*http://thomas.loc.gov/cgi-bin/query/z?c111:h.r.4173:*)"

36. U.S. Department of the Treasury, "Bureau of Consumer Financial Protection (CFPB) (*http://www.treasury.gov/initiatives/pages/cfpb.aspx*)"

37. Ari Berman, The Nation, "The Bank Lobby Steps Up Its Attack on Elizabeth Warren (*http://www.thenation.com/article/161069/bank-lobby-steps-its-attack-elizabeth-warren*)," June 1, 2011

38. Stanford Encyclopedia of Philosophy, "Privacy (*http://plato.stanford.edu/entries/privacy/*)," May 14, 2002

39. Wikipedia, "European Convention on Human Rights (*http://en.wikipedia.org/wiki/european_convention_on_human_rights*)"

40. Hellenic Resources Network, Council of Europe, "The European Convention on Human Rights and its Five Protocols, (*http://www.hri.org/docs/echr50.html#c.seci*)" November 1950

41. Electronic Privacy Information Center, "EU Data Protection Directive (*http://epic.org/privacy/intl/eu_data_protection_directive.html*)"

42. OCEG, "EU Telecommunications Privacy Directive (1997) (*http://www.oceg.org/view/15556*)"

43. Official Journal of the European Communities, "Directive 2002/58/EC of the European Parliament and of the Council of 12 July 2002 (*http://eur-lex.europa.eu/lexuriserv/lexuriserv.do?uri=oj:l:2006:105:0054:0063:en:pdf*)"

44. Wikipedia, "Directive on Privacy and Electronic Communications (*http://en.wikipedia.org/wiki/directive_on_privacy_and_electronic_communications*)"

45. Official Journal of the European Union, "Directive 2006/24/EC of the European Parliament and of the Council of 15 March 2006 (*http://eur-lex.europa.eu/lexuriserv/lexuriserv.do?uri=oj:l:2006:105:0054:0063:en:pdf*)"

46. The Register, "Data Retention Directive receives rubber stamp (*http://www.theregister.co.uk/2006/02/24/data_retention_directive_ratified/*)," February 24, 2006

47. Deutsche Welle, "EU data protection authority condemns data retention directive (*http://www.dw-world.de/dw/article/0,,15120172,00.html*)," May 31, 2011

48. Eddan Katz, Electronic Frontier Foundation, "The Beginning of the End of Data Retention (*http://www.eff.org/deeplinks/2010/03/beginning-end-data-retention*)," March 10, 2010

49. Wikipedia, "Data Protection Directive (*http://en.wikipedia.org/wiki/data_protection_directive*)"

50. IT Law Wiki, "Safe Harbor Agreement (*http://itlaw.wikia.com/wiki/safe_harbor_agreement*)"

51. TRUSTe, "EU Safe Harbor (*http://www.truste.com/privacy_seals_and_services/enterprise_privacy/eu_safe_harbor_seal.html*)"

52. Global Internet Liberty Campaign, "Privacy and Human Rights: An International Survey of Privacy Laws and Practice (*http://gilc.org/privacy/survey/intro.html*)"

53. APEC, "APEC Launches new Cross-border Data Privacy Initiative (*http://www.apec.org/en/press/news-releases/2010/0716_ecsg_cpea.aspx*)," July 16, 2010

54. Larry Dignan, ZDNet, "The cost of doing business in China: Privacy (*http://www.zdnet.com/blog/btl/the-cost-of-doing-business-in-china-privacy/10277*)," October 2, 2008

55. The Economist, "The long march to privacy (*http://www.economist.com/node/5389362?story_id=5389362*)," January 12, 2006

56. Alexei Oreskovic and Edwin Chan, Huffpost Tech, "Google: Gmail Hack Likely from China Cyberattackers (*http://www.huffingtonpost.com/2011/06/01/google-gmail-hack-china_n_869995.html*)," June 1, 2011

57. Ariel Silverstone, The Security Blog, "International Privacy Laws and International Security Breach Laws (*http://arielsilverstone.com/resources/international-privacy/*)," February 7, 2011

58. Wikipedia, "USA Patriot Act (*http://en.wikipedia.org/wiki/usa_patriot_act*)"

59. AFX News Limited, Forbes, "French parliament adopts tough anti-terrorism law (*http://www.forbes.com/feeds/afx/2005/12/22/afx2410169.html*)," December 12, 2005

60. Human Rights Watch, "UK: New Terrorism Law Fundamentally Flawed (*http://www.hrw.org/en/news/2005/03/14/uk-new-terrorism-law-fundamentally-flawed*)," March 14, 2005

61. Liberty, "Summary of the Prevention of Terrorism Act 2005 (*http://www.liberty-human-rights.org.uk/policy/reports/prevention-of-terrorism-act-2005-summary.pdf*)," May 2005

62. Ned Millis, eHow, "The Counter Terrorism Act 2008 (*http://www.ehow.com/facts_6770131_counter-terrorism-act-2008.html*)," July 24, 2010

63. Wikipedia, "Canadian Anti-Terrorism Act (*http://en.wikipedia.org/wiki/canadian_anti-terrorism_act*)"

64. Steven Lee Myers, The New York Times, "Rights Abuses Extend Across Middle East, Report Says (*http://www.nytimes.com/2011/04/09/world/middleeast/09rights.html?_r=2*)," April 8, 2011

65. Wikipedia, "List of terrorist incidents (*http://en.wikipedia.org/wiki/list_of_terrorist_incidents*)_"

66. Ann Cavoukian, Ph.D., Privacy by Design, The 7 Foundational Principles (*http://www.ipc.on.ca/images/resources/pbd-law-policy.pdf*)

67. James C. Duff, Report of the Director of the Administrative Office of the United States Courts, "Applications for Orders Authorizing or Approving the Interception of Wire, Oral, or Electronic Communications," April, 2010

68. Nigel Waters, University of New South Wales Faculty of Law Research Series 2008, Paper 59, "The APEC Asia-Pacific Privacy Initiative—a new route to effective data protection or a trojan horse for self-regulation? (*http://law.bepress.com/unswwps/flrps08/art59/*)," July 2008

69. David L. Baumer, Julia B. Earp, and J.C. Poindexter, College of Management, North Carolina State University, Raleigh, NC, "Internet Privacy Law: A Comparison between the United States and the European Union (*http://www.mendeley.com/research/internet-privacy-law-comparison-united-states-european-union-6/*)"

70. Hal Roberts, John Palfrey, "The EU Data Retention Directive in an Era of Internet Surveillance (*http://www.access-controlled.net/wp-content/pdfs/chapter-3.pdf*)"

71. Mozelle W. Thompson, Peder van Wagonen Magee, Privacy Regulation, "US/EU Safe Harbor Agreement: What It Is and What It Says About the Future of Cross Border Data Protection (*http://www.ftc.gov/speeches/thompson/thompsonsafehar bor.pdf*)," Spring 2003

72. Preliminary FTC Staff Report, "Protecting Consumer Privacy in an Era of Rapid Change (*http://www.ftc.gov/os/2010/12/101201privacyreport.pdf*)," December 2010

73. Detlev Zwick, Nikhilesh Dholakia, "Models of Privacy in the Digital Age: Implications for Marketing and E-Commerce (*http://ritim.cba.uri.edu/working%20pa pers/privacy-models-paper%5b1%5d.pdf*)," September 7, 1999

74. Nolan M. Goldberg, Micah W. Miller, National Law Journal Website, "The practice of law in the age of Big Data (*http://www.law.com/jsp/nlj/pubarticlenlj.jsp?id= 1202489457214&the_practice_of_law_in_the_age_of_big_data*)"

75. Lauren B. Movius, Nathalie Krup, International Journal of Communication 3 (2009), 169-187, "U.S. and EU Privacy Policy: Comparison of Regulatory Approaches (*http://ijoc.org/ojs/index.php/ijoc/article/viewfile/405/305*)"

76. Christopher Cwalina, Reed Smith, "U.S. Privacy Legislative and Regulatory Update (*http://www.adlawbyrequest.com/uploads/file/us%20privacy%20legislative %20and%20regulatory%20update.pdf*)"

77. Frank La Rue, United Nations General Assembly, Human Rights Council, "Report of the Special Rapporteur on the promotion and protection of the right to freedom of opinion and expression (*http://www2.ohchr.org/english/bodies/hrcouncil/docs/ 17session/a.hrc.17.27_en.pdf*)"

CHAPTER 4

The Players

Wherever you go, whatever you do, anywhere in this world, some "thing" is tracking you. Your laptop, and other personal devices, like an iPad, Smartphone, or Blackberry, all play a role, and contribute to building a very detailed dossier of your likes, concerns, preferred airlines, favorite vacation spots, how much money you spend, political affiliations, who you're friends with, the magazines you subscribe to, the make and model of the car you drive, the kinds of foods you buy, the list goes on. There are now RFID chips (*http://dvice.com/archives/2011/04/no-more-stealin.php*) in hotel towels and bathrobes to dissuade you from taking them with you while your in-room mini bar collects information about every item you've consumed (to ensure that it's properly stocked for your next visit). That convenient E-ZPass (*http://en.wikipedia.org/wiki/e-zpass*) not only makes your commute easier, but it also helps to provide an accurate picture of your whereabouts on any given day, at any given time, as do all the video cameras installed at ATMs, in stores, banks, and gas stations, on highways, and at traffic intersections. Your car collects information (*http://www.aclu-wa.org/news/my-car-my-pri vacy-bill-becomes-law*) about you—from your location, speed, steering, brake use, and driving patterns. Although your home may be your castle, it is not, in the world we now live in, impenetrable. Google Maps provides (*http://searchengineland.com/google -street-view-scorecard-55487*) a very accurate and detailed picture of it, and in the course of getting that picture, if you happened to have had an unencrypted Wi-Fi network, scooped up personal (*http://www.priv.gc.ca/media/nr-c/2010/let_101019_e.cfm*) data as well. You may be aware of all the digital tracking that is going on by the Internet giants (Google, Facebook, and the rest), but with almost 40 (*http://press.pandasecurity .com/wp-content/uploads/2011/07/pandalabs-report-q2-2011.pdf*) percent of PCs worldwide infected with some form of malware that can gather information and send it back to their authors, that may be the least of your worries.

Some would say that we live in a dataveillance society, where our actions and communications are systematically monitored. Remarkably, that term was coined in 1987 (*http: //www.rogerclarke.com/dv/cacm88.html*) by Roger Clarke, long before personal devices and the Internet of Things (*http://en.wikipedia.org/wiki/internet_of_things*) came into being and more than two decades before the Wall Street Journal's landmark series (*http://online.wsj.com/article/sb10001424052748703940904575395073512989404 .html?mod=what_they_know*) on "What they Know" which took an in depth look at the business of Internet spying. Surveillance, spying, eavesdropping, and tracking are words used to describe the constant monitoring of our lives by journalists, pundits, and authors (such as ourselves).

But does this truly characterize the world in which we live? Digitization, by its very nature, makes surveillance a permanent part of our lives. It is now very easy to passively (and automatically) collect data that documents the minutiae of our lives and, with or without our cooperation, store it. Our smart phones and other devices are more effective collectors of individual information than the KGB or Stasi, the most feared security agencies of the Cold War era. And this data we create is often copied and sold to third parties for unintended, at least from our perspective, purposes.

There are many players, including governments, involved in the ongoing privacy debate which at its core asks this question (*http://www.businessweek.com/technology/content/ jan2011/tc20110113_703365.htm*): is your personal information property or a basic human right? If it is property, than each one of us can trade it for all kinds of things and once we do, we cannot have an expectation that the information remains private. If it's a basic human right, than we cannot negotiate it away. While the jury is still out, we believe that the answer will lie somewhere in between, informed by the politics of where you live (how's that for clarity?).

Certainly, in the U.S., personal information is treated like property while other regions and countries regard it more as a constitutional right (see Chapter 2 and Chapter 3). To join Facebook, we provide personal information about ourselves, we invite family and friends to join, and in turn they provide their personal information. Then we share things we like, things we hate, things that make us sad or glad, all documented by our favorite photos. All of this stuff is digitally saved and associated specifically with us, representing a gold mine to private and public sectors; there is money to be made, behavior to be tracked, intellectual property to be protected, health risks to be monitored, political affiliations to be leveraged, and terrorist and criminals (*http://blogs.for bes.com/kashmirhill/2011/08/09/will-london-riots-be-the-turning-point-for-facial-recog nition-as-crime-fighting-tool/*) to be watched. The collection and use of our personal data was never just about advertising; it's about everything.

The way in which we live has changed forever. Devices have made our lives easier and we now live online for work and for play. Traditional industries, like print media, and businesses, like Borders, have been replaced by electronic publishing, like Ebooks, and commerce sites, like Amazon. The Internet is here to stay, and technologically and socially speaking, it is a singular disruptive force—one which individuals, companies, and organizations of all kinds must reckon with.

As with all controversial and contentious issues, the privacy debate is chocked full of competing agendas. The players, in singular and as groups, all have stakes in privacy-related regulatory actions and how those actions are monitored and enforced. There are privacy watchdog groups seeking more comprehensive and restrictive privacy legislation; there are large collectors and holders of personal data who argue for self-regulation; and there are users of data who analyze it to discover all sorts of things (for the greater good, to make money, for national or commercial espionage, or simply to commit crimes). Countries and regions, and their respective governments, have their own agendas—some maintaining that privacy definitions should be more restrictive, giving individuals much more control over their information, while others seek to strip privacy from their citizens, constantly watching and monitoring to restrict speech, prevent uprisings, or identify potential terrorists or criminals. Even within a single government, it is not unusual to see competing visions of privacy from different branches or agencies.

We, or our personal information (however you might characterize it), are at the center of a privacy battle, caught in a tug-of-war between these various groups and players. After all, it is our information they are all fighting about. How we align ourselves with the various privacy movements depends heavily upon our worldview. But make no mistake, all the players have huge stakes in ensuring that our expectation of privacy aligns with theirs. To understand the underlying issues, one must first understand the motivations driving the players.

Meet the Players

While there are all kinds of privacy players weighing in on whether one should be fearful or sanguine about the state of privacy today, they can be categorized into four distinct groups:

- **Data Collectors**. Whenever you use a personal digital device, such as a PC or cell phone (whether at work or at play), you generate data. You also generate data by intersecting with technology (that you don't own but still collects data about you), like RFID tags, loyalty and credit card readers, and CCTV cameras (located in public and private spaces). All of this data is collected by someone (or multiple someones) for some purpose, with or without your consent. Most often, that information is then sold or rented to third parties or as data sets that can be combined (aggregated) with other data sets.

- **Data Markets (the Aggregators)**. Data markets (*http://www.readwriteweb.com/ archives/on_data_markets_and_their_evolution.php*) are platforms where users (*http://www.readwriteweb.com/archives/where_to_find_open_data_on_the.php*) (individuals, marketing organizations or others, companies, and government agencies) may search for specific data sets that meet their needs and then download them (either free or for a fee, depending on the data set).

- **Data Users**. These are the people or organizations that buy or get free access to data, usually through applications (social media monitoring, retail analytics, customer relationship management, demand monitoring, inventory management, etc.). For example, if you've ever looked someone (or yourself) up on Spokeo (*http://www.spoke.com/*), you are working with a number of data sets that have been combined by Spokeo to provide that profile.

- **Data Monitors/Protectors**. There are a host of agencies and organizations that monitor privacy issues from various points of view and others that are involved in self-regulatory policies and enforcement for various industries or functions.

For each of these groups, the intrinsic value that our personal information represents may be quite different but in all cases, it is significant. Certainly, any company or person engaged in advertising would attest to that. But while advertising may be at the center of the privacy debate, there are all kinds of players who derive considerable value from our personal information. That being the case, online advertising has pushed the technology envelope for creating and maintaining detailed digital profiles (behavioral and otherwise) of each and every one of us.

A (Very) Brief History of Online Advertising

Online advertising, although very different in terms of scope and types, follows the same business model as offline advertising. It is quite simple: "... consumers are paid with content and services to receive advertising messages and advertisers pay to send these messages."[1] Theoretically, any website delivers content and services in some form or another, so any website (and the company or individual behind it) could include paid advertising on its pages and profit from it. For advertisers, this represents a new frontier to explore with costs that are far less than traditional venues, along with the intriguing possibility of gathering much more information about their targeted audiences which translates into more effective advertising and ultimately, more sales.

It all began in 1994, when HotWired (*http://en.wikipedia.org/wiki/hotwired*), the first commercial web magazine, displayed an AT&T banner ad which was the first of its kind. Until then, advertising was limited to offline publications, such as magazines and newspapers, store displays, product packaging, television, radio, telephone, and of course, the universally despised direct mail pieces that filled up all of our mailboxes. At that point, most of the web consisted of static content and was viewed as just another (new) advertising channel.

AT&T bought the ad based on the number of impressions (as in the number of individuals who viewed the ad). This quickly evolved into the cost per 1,000 views (CPM) and then in 1996, Proctor & Gamble negotiated a deal with Yahoo! (*http://www.yahoo.com/*) where ads would be paid on a cost-per-click (CPC) basis. This is very similar to the payment method employed by direct marketing houses and telemarketing organi-

---

1. David S. Evans, University College London and University of Chicago, "The Online Advertising Industry: Economics, Evolution, and Privacy," April 2009, pg. 9

zations. Up until 2008, this was the standard way in which online advertising fees were based.[2]

Thus, a very large and profitable cottage industry was born, intent on creating and using technology to track (and record) how individuals navigated the web, what they looked at, and what they bought as well as a plethora of companies that operated on the publishing or advertising sides to facilitate the creation, placement, and tracking (including ROI) of ads based on targeted profiles. At the forefront of all of this was tracking technology (simple by today's standards) designed to follow the user around and essentially, document his (or her) every digital move. Today, ETags (*http://en.wikipedia.org/wiki/http_etag*), cookies (*http://www.prestinaegele.com/technology-tracking-technology-in roads-create-consumer-backlash*), flash cookies, beacons (*http://online.wsj.com/article/sb10001424052748703940904575395073512989404.html?mod=what_they_know*), supercookies, and history stealing (*http://online.wsj.com/article/sb10001424053111903480904576508382675931492.html*) are all employed to track and collect what you do online from any device by the sites you visit and from unknown third parties (one step removed, such as an ad on a page that you visit). Location tracking (*http://www.computerworld.com/s/article/9215033/big_data_to_drive_a_surveil lance_society?source=ctwnle_nlt_pm_2011-03-24*), where geo-location data generated from cell phones can be used to triangulate your location at any given time, is also on the rise as is its use in targeted mobile advertising. All of this information can be tied directly back to you; the days of assuming anonymity on the web are over.

From an advertising perspective, the Internet is unique in the amount of information it can generate and collect about individuals and groups of individuals which leads to higher quality and more targeted segmentation (*http://www.marketingteacher.com/les son-store/lesson-segmentation.html*) (creating a target audience based on a selected set of variables). The key here is that the more you are able to accurately target a prospective buyer in terms of his behavior (i.e., behavioral advertising (*http://www.seochat.com/c/ a/website-marketing-help/how-and-why-behavioral-advertising-works/*)) the better your return (click through and conversion rates go up). Added to that, technology has advanced to such an extent that ads can be placed in near real-time. For example, if you are on an orthopedic site reading about a specific knee brace and then go to another website, a banner ad pops up with an ad for knee braces (just seconds later). Or you receive a 50 percent off coupon on your mobile device for the restaurant you are walking by. Finally, traditional offline advertising mediums are either dying (print magazines and newspapers) or waning (network television and radio) as consumers increasingly favor digital and streaming media (*http://en.wikipedia.org/wiki/streaming_media*) as well as hanging out on social media sites, all premier publishing venues for advertisers.

From a publishing perspective, pretty much any site can incorporate advertising into its business model as a revenue channel. The rise of advertising intermediaries—those

---

2. David S. Evans, University College London and University of Chicago, "The Online Advertising Industry: Economics, Evolution, and Privacy," April 2009, pg. 5

companies that broker ad buys or placements for a fee (from either the advertisers or publishers perspective) and networks that do the same but work at an aggregated level —have made it possible for even small businesses, organizations, and blogs to create a substantial advertising revenue stream. Of course, this entire ecosystem is supported by the data suppliers and markets that deliver detailed information about each one of us. It goes without saying (but we will) that their most important asset is everything they individually and collectively know about us.

However you cut it, online advertising (made up of search, banner and video ads, classifieds, rich media, lead generation, sponsorships, and email) is big business. A recent forecast (*http://techcrunch.com/2011/06/08/online-ad-spending-31-billion/*), courtesy of eMarketer, estimates that online ad spending will reach $31.3 billion in 2011 (with Google taking the lion's share (*http://investor.google.com/financial/tables.html*)), up 20 percent from last year, and is projected to reach $50 billion by 2015. It accounts for nearly 20 percent of the major media dollar spend in the U.S. this year and is expected to make up almost 28 percent of the total spend by 2015. So while Google, Twitter, Facebook, LinkedIn, Yahoo, and Foursquare may offer diverse services to their users, their revenue and valuations are driven by the data they collect and the multi-billion dollar value it represents to advertisers.

When it comes to advertising and privacy, it could be argued that advertisers don't care about what we do or where we go, they do not act as moral arbiters on our lives. They are simply interested in one thing: getting us to buy what they're selling. If a privacy debate is framed with this in mind, it is easy to say that the impact is rather benign: what are a few more targeted ads delivered to your mobile when you're near a particular store or served up to you when you're surfing for a specific item? What's the harm in trading your information for a specific service? Here's the rub: the information collected about us is not just used by advertisers to sell stuff to us. It's used for myriad purposes, none of which we have control over.

Intellectual Property Rights, Trusted Computing, and Privacy

While the advertising industry is interested in collecting data to get us to buy something, certain sectors heavily dependent on the protection of intellectual property (IP), like the recording, publishing, television, movie, and software industries, are far more interested in what we do with the items *after* we buy them. As we've said before, the digital age has been a disruptive force and while the advertising industry has leveraged it to vigorously pursue their business model, other industries have watched theirs crumble.

The free and easy digitization of all kinds of "property" whether it is music, movies, books, or video, has caused some powerful groups, like the Recording Industry Association of America (RIAA (*http://www.riaa.com/*)), the Motion Picture Association of America (MPAA (*http://www.mpaa.org/*)), and their counterparts in the EU, to advocate for technology that protects their merchandise which strikes at the heart of the privacy debate. Essentially, they want to monitor, control, and in some cases, remove or delete their products on any devices we own to protect their intellectual property rights. To do this, they are enlisting the support of other parties, including hardware manufacturers, Internet Service Providers, the legislature, and law enforcement agencies. Most disturbing for privacy advocates, almost all of their approaches require the ability to uniquely identify and associate digital devices and their uses with its owner. We don't know about you, but we find this troubling at best and far more intrusive than anything the advertising industry has come up with. What exactly does purchasing and downloading, say an online book, really mean if someone can take it away from us without our permission (*http://www.engadget.com/2009/07/17/amazon-remotely-deletes-orwell -e-books-from-kindles-unpersons-r/*)?

Intellectual property law (*http://en.wikipedia.org/wiki/intellectual_property*) has been around, in some form or another, since the 1500's and unlike privacy, is explicitly granted in the U.S. Constitution (*http://law.jrank.org/pages/5722/copyright-history -copyright-law.html*) (Article 1, Section 8, Clause 8). It is designed to grant owners of intangible assets, like musical, literary, and artistic works, or discoveries and inventions, certain exclusive rights to that asset. In the U.S., there are laws and certain protections given to IP which can be broadly categorized into the following:

- **Trade secrets** are information that companies keep secret to gain a competitive advantage over others.
- **Copyrights** (*http://en.wikipedia.org/wiki/copyright*) are sets of rights granted to the creator of an original work for a limited (although historically, constantly expanding) period of time in exchange for public disclosure of the work. The "work" could be a book, play, sheet music, painting, photograph, sound recording, movie, or a computer program. The "rights" include the right to copy, distribute and adapt the work. There is also the Fair Use doctrine (*http://www.copyright.gov/fls/fl102 .html*) which allows for the reproduction of a work if it is used in commentary, critical reviews, research, parody, news reporting, etc.
- **Patents** (*http://en.wikipedia.org/wiki/patent*) are similar to copyrights in that they are a set of rights granted to an inventor for a period of time in exchange for public disclosure of the invention.

Essentially, intellectual property laws protect intangible assets from theft or piracy and certainly the digital age has brought into question just what those terms mean. The advent of file sharing, where music, video, movies, and documents are easily shared between devices, propelled by the rise (and then fall) of first generation peer-to-peer sharing networks, like Napster (*http://en.wikipedia.org/wiki/napster*), Grokster (*http:// en.wikipedia.org/wiki/grokster*), and Madster (*http://en.wikipedia.org/wiki/madster*), as well as the continued success of BitTorrent (*http://en.wikipedia.org/wiki/bittorrent*)- based sites like The Pirate Bay (*http://thepiratebay.org/*) has brought two ideologies into direct conflict: those who want to protect IP at all costs versus those who argue that the Internet by definition is designed to easily facilitate the sharing (as well as copying) of information between users.

To protect their IP, the recording industry went after Napster and Grokster as well as all commercial peer-to-peer networks. In 2005, it won a significant round as the Supreme Court found that "...file-sharing networks that intentionally profited by illegal distribution of music could be held liable for their actions."[3] This ruling caused most peer-to-peer networks to shut down or work out some sort of legal distribution agreement (for example, Apple's iTunes business model) with the record companies.

Of course, as in most things, money, specifically the perceived economic loss incurred by the sharing and copying of "pirated" files, formed the heart of this conflict. One of the more famous figures bandied about is "that 750,000 jobs and up to $250 billion a year could be lost in the U.S. economy thanks to IP infringement."[4] These statistics and others, like the Business Software Alliance's estimate that the U.S. piracy rate for business software is 20 percent or $9 billion in 2008 and the Motion Picture Association's estimate that its studios lost $6.1 billion to piracy in 2005, have been debunked by none other than the Government Accountability Office who came to this conclusion:

> "While experts and literature we reviewed provided different examples of effects on the U.S. economy, most observed that despite significant efforts, it is difficult, if not impossible, to quantify the net effect of counterfeiting and piracy on the economy as a whole... To determine the net effect, any positive effects of counterfeiting and piracy on the economy should be considered, as well as the negative effects."[5]

While estimates of the economic damage caused by piracy and counterfeiting were, and are, questionable, it did not stop these industries from lobbying and receiving legal digital copyright protection. The Digital Millennium Copyright Act (*http://www.copy right.gov/legislation/hr2281.pdf*) (DMCA, 1998) and the European Union Copyright Directive (*http://eur-lex.europa.eu/lexuriserv/lexuriserv.do?uri=celex:32001l0029:en: html*) (EUCD, 2001) implemented the World Intellectual Property Organization's (WIPO) Copyright Treaty (*http://www.wipo.int/treaties/en/ip/wct/trtdocs_wo033.html*) (1996) that specified the following:

- It was illegal to circumvent copyright technology (otherwise known as Digital Rights Management (*http://en.wikipedia.org/wiki/digital_rights_management*)) designed to protect materials. In other words, you (as in each and everyone one of us) cannot use available tools to "break" copyright and share and copy files, etc.

3. Kenneth C. Laudon & Jane Price Laudon, Management Information Systems: Managing the Digital Firm, "Chapter 4: Ethical and Social Issues in Information Systems (*http://www.prenhall.com/behindthebook/0132304619/*)," April 2005, pg. 147

4. Nate Anderson, arsTechnica, "U.S. Government finally admits most piracy estimates are bogus," August 2010

5. GAO Report to Congressional Committees, "Intellectual Property: Observations on Efforts to Quantify the Economic Effects of Counterfeit and Pirated Goods," April 2010, pg. 27

- Internet Service Providers (ISPs) are required to take down the hosted sites of copyright infringers once they are made aware of the problem. In others words, ISPs are the copyright police and the tops ones are already on board, including (*http://epic.org/privacy/copyright/epic-wipo-testimony-698.html*) Comcast, Cablevision, Verizon, and Time Warner Cable.

The concept of digital rights management (DRM) is quite simple: it is technology used by IP holders (publishers, hardware and software manufacturers, etc.) to control access to their copyright materials on digital devices. Out of the desire for an advanced DRM system, Microsoft, Intel, IBM, HP, and AMD got together and formed the Trusted Computing Group (*http://www.trustedcomputinggroup.org/*) (TCG). The goal of this group was to develop a standard for a more secure PC or as Ross Anderson puts it:

> "[It] provides a computing platform on which you can't tamper with the application software, and where these applications can communicate securely with their authors and with each other. The original motivation was *digital rights management* (*http://www .theregister.co.uk/content/archive/23387.html*) (DRM): Disney will be able to sell you DVDs that will decrypt and run on a TC platform, but which you won't be able to copy. The music industry will be able to sell you music downloads that you won't be able to swap. They will be able to sell you CDs that you'll only be able to play three times, or only on your birthday. All sorts of new marketing possibilities will open up."[6]

The TCG introduced the Trusted Platform Module (*http://en.wikipedia.org/wiki/trusted _platform_module*) (TPM—yes, we love acronyms as much as you do!) which is a specification and also a modifier for hardware that implements that specification, like the TPM chip. You may also know the chip by another name, the Fritz chip. It was named in honor of Senator Fritz Hollings of South Carolina who wanted the chip in pretty much every device we own:

> "Hollings' bill... would require any device that can 'retrieve or access copyrighted works in digital form' to include a federally mandated copy protection system... That covers not just your next iPod or Windows Media Player, but just about every digital device with a screen, a printer, an audio jack, a disk drive, a memory stick, or several input/ output devices yet to be invented. Your computer, your camera, your car stereo."[7]

The TCG, TPM, and Fritz chip have all been met with a great deal of controversy. Besides the concern that TPM and the chip (which is now used by almost all the notable PC and Notebook manufacturers (*http://en.wikipedia.org/wiki/trusted_platform_mod ule#spread*)) would cause consumers to lose all anonymity in online transactions, some have argued that the TCG members have, by virtue of their alliance, made themselves far more powerful to the point of monopolistic and unfair business practices. Others have pointed out that whoever controls the infrastructure becomes a single, powerful point of control. Anderson equates this to making everyone use the same bank, lawyer,

---

6. Ross Anderson, "Trusted Computing Frequently Asked Questions (*http://en.wikipedia.org/wiki/ european_union_copyright_directive*)," August 2003

7. Paul Boutin, Salon, "U.S. prepares to invade your hard drive (*http://www.salon.com/technology/ feature/2002/03/29/hollings_bill/*)," March 29, 2002

or accountant.[8] There is also the issue of remote censorship as digital objects can be easily removed from any device—without users' permission. Amazon certainly illustrated the power of TPM when it removed two of George Orwell's books, Animal Farm and 1984, from customers' Kindles:

> "This is precisely the functional equivalent of Barnes & Noble -- or Amazon itself for that matter -- using a crowbar or lock pick to break into your home or business, then stealing back a previous physical book purchase, replacing it with the equivalent value in cash," said privacy advocate Lauren Weinstein.[9]

Outside of the monumental potential for abuse by large corporations and governments (and all of their agencies), when fully implemented, TPM essentially strips us of any expectation of privacy or anonymity. It uniquely identifies every device, ties that device to its owner(s), and then monitors and reports back on what is read, written, watched, or listened to. Do we really want any government or corporation to be able to easily monitor and decide what we should or should not be reading or what software we are allowed to use on our devices? Now, although the Fritz chip can be found in most PCs, it has been banned in China. For some odd reason, the Chinese have no interest in giving U.S. corporations (or their government) the ability to turn off the operating system for every computer connected to the Internet.

While the EU is pushing for a right to be forgotten, it appears that powerful IP players are pushing for the right to know everything about what we do with their IP. Historically, this has never been the intent of copyright law, as Marc Rotenberg noted in a Senate Subcommittee hearing way back in 1998:

> "Traditionally, copyright law has not posed a particular problem for privacy protection. Readers, listeners and viewers have always enjoyed very high levels of privacy, by practice if not by law, without any threat to the interests of copyright holders. Copyright grants certain rights to copyright holders, but these rights do not include the right to know the identity of the copyright user."[10]

Better yet, it appears that we no longer own our digital assets as copyright holders, or those acting in their interests, can remove it. Instead, we are merely renters but with far fewer rights than renters of physical property.

---

8. Ross Anderson, "Trusted Computing Frequently Asked Questions (*http://en.wikipedia.org/wiki/european _union_copyright_directive*)," August 2003

9. Tomas Claburn, InformationWeek, "Amazon Says It Will Stop Deleting Kindle Books (*http://www .informationweek.com/news/personal-tech/digital-content/218501227*)," July 17,2009

10. Testimony and Statement (*http://epic.org/privacy/copyright/epic-wipo-testimony-698.html*) for the Record of Marc Rotenberg, Director, Electronic Privacy Information Center Adjunct Professor, Georgetown University Law Center Senior Lecturer, Washington College of Law, on H.R. 2281. The WIPO Copyright Treaties Implementation Act and Privacy Issues, Before the Subcommittee on Telecommunications, Trade, and Consumer Protection, Committee on Commerce, U.S. House of Representatives, June 5, 1998

It is interesting to note that while individuals and their use of IP assets have been under tremendous scrutiny, a far more insidious threat has been, until recently, flying under the radar: the theft of patents, trade secrets, and copyright assets due to cyber attacks whose scope, sophistication, and targets suggest that this is the work of nation states, not individual hackers. A recent study by McAfee uncovered that the networks of "72 organizations including the United Nations, governments and companies around the world had been infiltrated"[11] which is considered to be "... the biggest transfer of wealth in terms of intellectual property in history."[12] Our point is this: instead of focusing on individuals, perhaps the government, large IP holders, their assorted lobbyists, and industry groups should be turning their attention to this much larger threat to intellectual property.

Pushing the Privacy Envelope All the Way to the Bank

While the IP stakeholders have been busy redefining "privacy" for their own ends, Google, Yahoo, Facebook, and others have been equally busy making billions of dollars collecting our data and using it for targeted advertising. Of course, any company or organization that collects data can offer it for sale or free. Certainly, federal (*http:// explore.data.gov/*) and state agencies, in their move toward a more open and transparent government, have made many comprehensive data sets available for public use (ranging from census to weather to loan and property information). Sometimes this data is sold, as illustrated by the state of Florida (*http://www.dailymail.co.uk/news/article-2017087/ florida-makes-63m-selling-names-addresses-dates-birth-lists-vehicles-people-drive .html*) who made $63 million dollars last year by selling DMV information (including name, date of birth, and type of vehicle driven) to companies like Lexus Nexus and Shadow Soft. Sometimes this data is made available due to state transparency laws, as illustrated by Florida's public display of mug shots on government websites. This action formed the basis of several businesses (*http://www.wired.com/threatlevel/2011/08/mug shots/*), the most lucrative being one that helps you remove your arrest information from public websites.

It is, however, the big companies and their ecosystems that are most responsible for pushing the privacy envelope and most of them are involved, in one way or another, with social networking (*http://www.mercurynews.com/business/ci_18349132?source= rss*) (like Google, Yahoo, Facebook, Twitter, Groupon, LinkedIn, and Zynga). These companies are in the primary business of data: collecting, sharing, and even selling users' information. Most of them, unsurprisingly, have also pushed the privacy envelope:

---

11. Jim Finkle, msnbc.com, "Biggest-ever series of cyber attacks uncovered, UN hit (*http://www.msnbc.msn .com/id/43998147/ns/technology_and_science-security/#.tjlblyixg4q*)," August 3, 2011

12. Jim Finkle, msnbc.com, "Biggest-ever series of cyber attacks uncovered, UN hit (*http://www.msnbc.msn .com/id/43998147/ns/technology_and_science-security/#.tjlblyixg4q*)," August 3, 2011

"... in the past year, Silicon Valley firms have seen a bevy of Web companies like them swept into investigations for consumer protection violations and fraud... Last week, Internet radio site Pandora revealed that it was called into a broad federal grand jury investigation into the alleged illegal sharing of user data by a number of companies that create apps for iPhone and Android devices. Days earlier, Google settled with the Federal Trade Commission on charges it exposed data through its Buzz social networking application without the permission of users. Last year, Twitter settled with the agency after an investigation found the site's loose security allowed hackers to access user information." [13]

These giants are the owners of a treasure trove of personal information. How did they collect it? Much of it was (and continues to be), given away by individuals in the course of interacting with each other on these sites. Some of it was obtained through the employment of digital tracking, known or not, as shown by the Wall Street Journal who conducted an experiment to explore the use of digital tracking. In this experiment, the Journal discovered that 50 of the most popular sites (representing 40 percent of all web pages viewed by Americans) placed a total of 3,180 tracking devices on the Journal's test computer (in a simulation of a normal user surfing sites, buying goods, and interacting with others via social networks). Most of these devices were unknown to the user.[14] Additionally, the Journal discovered that Flash cookies "... can also be used by data collectors to re-install regular cookies that a user has deleted. This can circumvent a user's attempt to avoid being tracked online."[15] A Stanford study (*http://www.leader post.com/technology/online+privacy+tools+fail+prevent+tracking+study+warns/ 5144051/story.html*) also found that half of the 64 online advertising companies (including Goggle, Yahoo, AOL, and Microsoft) it examined continued tracking even when do not track options were activated. So even if we, as users, are proactive about privacy it does not follow that the collectors will be prevented from gathering information about us.

Adherence to privacy policies and practices are also under fire. Facebook is well known for its questionable privacy policies which are based on defaulting user sharing to a public option (although Google's launch of Google+, which defaults user sharing to a private option, has caused Facebook to change some of its practices). Last year, it was revealed (*http://online.wsj.com/article/ sb10001424052702304410504575560640816473962.html?mod=wsj_hpp_middletop stories*) that third party Facebook applications were able to collect personally identifi-

---

13. Cecilia Kang, The Washington Post, "Web firms face increased federal scrutiny over Internet privacy (*http://www.washingtonpost.com/business/economy/web-firms-face-increased-federal -scrutiny-over-internet-privacy/2011/04/06/afvrep1c_story.html*)," April 8, 2011

14. Julia Angwin, Wall Street Journal, "The Web's New Gold Mine: Your Secrets (*http://online.wsj.com/ article/sb10001424052748703940904575395073512989404.html?mod=what_they_know*)," July 30, 2010

15. Julia Angwin, Wall Street Journal, "The Web's New Gold Mine: Your Secrets (*http://online.wsj.com/ article/sb10001424052748703940904575395073512989404.html?mod=what_they_know*)," July 30, 2010

---

able information for Facebook users, specifically user ID numbers that could "…be used to look up the user's real name and sometimes other information users have made public, and potentially tie it to their activity inside the apps."[16] This year Facebook renewed concerns about its privacy policies with the release of its Tag Suggestions feature (*http://www.smh.com.au/technology/technology-news/facebook-facial-recogni tion-technology-sparks-renewed-privacy-concerns-20110608-1fs3n.html*) based on facial recognition technology that would enable its users to more easily identify and label friends and acquaintances who appear in their posted photos. The reason for concern is that this feature was offered as an opt out, meaning that users would have to manually go into their settings and turn it off.

The issue of opting out versus opting in for any feature or service is central to the privacy debate. Proponents argue that the use of opt out erodes users' privacy without their knowledge and enables collectors to collect even more personal information, pushing the privacy envelope even further. So what privacy concerns you might have had prior to the introduction of a new feature or service, becomes a social norm because "everyone is doing it." Most collectors caught using opt out argue that the loss of privacy was accidental as there was no intent to invade one's privacy but merely to make it easier to adopt a new great feature. In our view, that is a dubious claim at best given the clear economic benefits to the collector.

Should you think this type of behavior is limited to Facebook, think again. After going public, LinkedIn announced in its blog (*http://blog.linkedin.com/2011/06/10/privacy -policy-changes/*) that it would allow advertisers to include us in ads if we recommended their product or service. Specifically, buried within each member's account settings profile page it described its new service this way:

> *"LinkedIn may sometimes pair an advertiser's message with social content from LinkedIn's network in order to make the ad more relevant. When LinkedIn members recommend people and services, follow companies, or take other actions, their name/photo may show up in related ads shown to you. Conversely, when you take these actions on LinkedIn, your name/ photo may show up in related ads shown to LinkedIn members. By providing social context, we make it easy for our members to learn about products and services that the LinkedIn network is interacting with."*

This feature was already turned on for all the LinkedIn members and required opting out to turn it off. More importantly, most members were unaware of this change until it was reported by the media (*http://www.businessinsider.com/fyi-linkedin-is-using-your -photo-and-your-actions-in-social-advertising-2011-7*). Groupon also recently announced (*http://www.washingtonpost.com/blogs/post-tech/post/groupon-changes-pri vacy-policy-to-collect-share-more-information/2011/07/10/giqanxx67h_blog.html*) a significant change in its privacy policy in an email to all its users. It will now be collecting

---

16. Geoffrey A. Fowler, Wall Street Journal, "More Questions for Wall Street (*http://online.wsj.com/article/ sb10001424052702304410504575560640816473962.html?mod=wsj_hpp_middletopstories*)," October 18, 2010

more information about its users to share with partners and using geo-location information to market to them.

If your business model is predicated on the collection and ownership of personal information that results in a revenue stream worth billions of dollars, it stands to reason that you view this information as your property. As such, you can buy it, rent it, and sell it. It is also in your best interest to discover, via trackers, services, or new features, as much as you can about the people who use your site. After all, the more targeted the profile the more valuable it becomes to the advertiser. For these companies, stringent privacy regulations would curb their ability to make money and in their words, "deprive consumers from advertisers' abilities to serve up more relevant ads." This is certainly the case lobbyists are making (*http://www.leaderpost.com/technology/online+privacy +tools+fail+prevent+tracking+study+warns/5144051/story.html*) for Google (spending $5.2 million in 2010), Yahoo ($2.2. million), Apple ($1.2 million) and Facebook ($350,000). While the first part of this argument makes economic sense, it is disingenuous to suggest that consumers, who have indicated through a number of surveys (*http: //www.google.com/hostednews/afp/article/aleqm5jm38cd0ygvdpxro1_dohxoq__-rw*) their growing disapproval (up to 86 percent) of tailored advertising, would feel deprived by less invasive advertising.

Unprecedented Access Further Erodes Privacy Expectations

From a privacy point of view, data markets and aggregators follow the collectors' play book. They also offer a treasure trove of personal information, but often on a much larger scale since they function as marketplace platforms where anyone can search and find data sets to fill almost any need while companies, organizations, and individuals can offer up their data sets for sale.

Data markets can be quite specific (focusing on a single market, for example), or quite broad (multiple subjects or audiences, sets of tracked behaviors or other variables, with historical performance and indicators, as examples). Thomson Reuters (*http://thom sonreuters.com/products_services/legal/legal_products/risk_fraud_investigations/*) offers data about the risk of doing business with an individual or a company; InfoChimps (*http://www.infochimps.com/*) offers a broad range of data sets; Gnip (*http://gnip.com/ sources*) is focused on social media feeds; Microsoft Azure (*https://datamarket.azure .com/*) offers data sets and services oriented toward (and from) its customers and partners; and Neilsen (*http://www.nielsen.com/us/en.html*) offers data sets and services oriented towards the industries it covers (media and entertainment, consumer packaged goods and retail, and telecom). There are also data markets that specialize in advertisers' interests, like Rapleaf (*https://www.rapleaf.com/people/rapleaf101*), Acxiom (*http:// www.acxiom.com/pages/home.aspx*), ChoicePoint (*http://en.wikipedia.org/wiki/choice point*) (now Reed Elsevier), Quantcast (*http://www.quantcast.com/*), and BluKai (*http: //www.bluekai.com/*), who provide targeted user profiles (including email addresses, resident addresses, names, income, social networks, and much more) through the aggregation of many data sets and the use of **tracking devices**. These are just a few of the markets out there: there are hundreds of companies that operate as middlemen for all kinds of data categories, many offering analytics and other services to help transform the data into information that can be acted upon (whether the action is to place an ad, determine the whereabouts of a person, ask for a charitable donation, predict where a crime may occur, or identify protestors in a march).

Just like the collectors, these players have little interest in comprehensive privacy regulations or guidelines as it does not serve their business models. For example, last year Rapleaf (*http://money.cnn.com/2010/10/21/technology/rapleaf/index.htm*) came under fire for linking user names and email addresses to specific social networking profiles and then selling that information to third parties. And, like Facebook, this was not the first time that Rapleaf was accused of privacy violations:

> "In 2007, CNET reported (*http://news.cnet.com/at-rapleaf,-your-personals-are-public/2100-1038_3-6205716.html*) that the company operated two other subsidiaries that secretly shared information with one another to create extremely detailed profiles about users -- including their social network affiliations. Rapleaf quickly responded by merging all of its businesses under one brand."[17]

But with data markets, privacy violations are not always willful or known. The number of data sets available for purchase or free are growing as fast as the underlying data that drives them. The markets make it easy to find and buy any number of data sets, which sets in motion the leakage of private information, as evidenced by a recent AT&T Research study of 120 of the most popular Internet sites which found that:

> "... fully 56 percent of the sites directly leak pieces of private information with this result growing to 75 percent if we also include leakage of a site userid. Sensitive search strings sent to healthcare Web sites and travel itineraries on flight reservation sites are leaked in 9 of the top 10 sites studied for each category."[18]

In a previous study, AT&T Research looked at how third parties can link personally identifiable information (PII) that is leaked by social networks with other user actions on that site and on other sites.[19] In other words, it is fairly easy to collect private information and link them to a specific individual as the study points out:

> "A well-known result in linking pieces of PII is that most Americans (87 percent) can be uniquely identified from a birth date, five-digit zip code, and gender."[20]

17. David Goldman, CNNMoney, "Rapleaf is selling your identity (*http://money.cnn.com/2010/10/21/technology/rapleaf/index.htm*)," October 21, 2010

18. Balanchander Krishnamurthy, Konstatin Naryshkin, Craig E. Wills, AT&T Labs and Worcester Polytechnic Institute, "Privacy leakage vs. Protection measures: the growing disconnect (*http://w2spconf.com/2011/papers/privacyvsprotection.pdf*)," 2011, pg. 1

19. Balanchander Krishnamurthy, Craig E. Wills, AT&T Labs and Worcester Polytechnic Institute, "On the Leakage of Personally Identifiable Information Via Online Social Networks (*http://portal.acm.org/citation.cfm?id=1672328*)," 2010, pg. 1

The emergence of new data analysis systems known collectively as "big data" have dramatically lowered the cost of merging and analyzing large data sets. These big data systems, including Hadoop (*http://hadoop.apache.org/*), S4 (*http://s4.io/*), CloudEra (*http://www.cloudera.com*), StreamInsight, (*http://www.microsoft.com/sqlserver/en/us/solutions-technologies/business-intelligence/complex-event-processing.aspx*) BackType (*http://www.backtype.com/*) (recently purchased by Twitter (*http://www.twitter.com*)) and our own PatternBuilders Analytics Framework (*http://patternbuilders.com/technology/platform.aspx*), make it relatively easy for companies and individuals to find, buy, and aggregate any number of data sets from any number of data markets, which, in turn, makes it that much easier to derive private information.

The more data you are able to collect and connect to other data sets, the easier it is to obtain what was thought to be private information and then tie that information to a specific individual. Once that link is made, you are then able to build a detailed profile, with multiple data sets providing you with more and more information. Certainly, a recent announcement by advertising giant WPP (*http://www.wpp.com/wpp/*) PLC about the launch of a new company, Xaxis (*http://online.wsj.com/article/sb10001424052702304447804576409562922859314.html#ixzz1qhf7phes*), may give many privacy advocates pause (it certainly did us) as it will manage:

> "... the world's largest database of profiles of individuals that includes demographic, financial, purchase, geographic and other information collected from their Web activities and brick-and-mortar transactions... WPP executives say Xaxis will have more than 500 million unique profiles, reaching virtually 100 percent of the population in markets where it operates."[21]

While WPP also points out that all this information is anonymous and that they will self-regulate, this much information about any one profile would make it fairly easy to attach a name, email address, and other personal identifiers.

In essence, data markets act as third party brokers of data sets. What happens after those sets are purchased and then used for any number of business or research purposes, is unknown. While the markets may be subject to ubiquitous privacy policies of the collectors and have their own privacy policies, it is not clear how data usage can be policed and enforced once the data changes hands. Anonymity may be promised, but as famously demonstrated by Netflix's (*http://www.pcworld.com/businesscenter/article/172373/new_irresponsible_netflix_contest_may_violate_customer_privacy.html*) research contest, through big data it is often easily broken.

20. Balanchander Krishnamurthy, Craig E. Wills, AT&T Labs and Worcester Polytechnic Institute, "On the Leakage of Personally Identifiable Information Via Online Social Networks (*http://portal.acm.org/citation.cfm?id=1672328*)," 2010, pg. 2

21. Emily Steel, Wall Street Journal, "WPP Ad Unit Has Your Profile (*http://online.wsj.com/article/sb10001424052702304447804576409562922859314.html#ixzz1qhf7phes*)," June 27, 2011

Letting the Genie Out of the Bottle

Much of the privacy debate focuses on the data, its collectors and markets. We are bombarded with information (as we have just shown) on how easy it is to track and collect data about us but equally important is the fact that, outside of advertising, there is a great deal unknown about how our data is, and could be, used. And while we understand what advertisers are doing with it, as Jeff Jonas said in a recent interview (*http://radar.oreilly.com/2011/04/jeff-jonas-data-privacy-control.html*):

> "The truth about data is once it's out there, it's hard to control."[22]

And there have been plenty of examples of the many ways in which our data is used—with or without our knowledge:

- The creepy application (*http://www.thinq.co.uk/2011/3/30/creepy-app-warns-end-privacy/*) that takes location information from every Tweet (for a Twitter user) or uploaded photo (for a Flickr user) and plots it on a map, which reveals hot spots around users' homes, workplaces, and other places they routinely visit.

- U.S. law enforcement officials that use GPS technology to track criminal suspects and parolees without their knowledge and without meeting the standards of wiretap laws or other laws regulating electronic surveillance because they "do not record conversations."[23]

- The iPhone Tracker (*http://petewarden.github.com/iphonetracker/*), developed by Peter Warden and Alasdair Allan, to show how the iPhone's unencrypted location history file (that holds more than a year of location data) can be used to provide a detailed picture of wherever you have been.

- The use of network analysis software employed by the Richmond, Virginia police department to analyze "... the social networks around suspects, such as dealings with employers, collection agencies, and the Department of Motor Vehicles. The goal... is to pull together a complete picture of suspects and their social circle."[24]

- The use of facial recognition technology (*http://www.usatoday.com/news/washington/2007-05-10-facial-recognition-terrorism_n.htm*) to quickly find terrorists and criminals using digital surveillance photos.

- The use of handheld facial recognition devices by more than a dozen law enforcement agencies where an officer can "snap a picture of a face from up to five feet away, or scan a person's irises from up to six inches away, and do an immediate search to see if there is a match with a database of people with criminal records."[25]

---

22. Jenn Webb, O'Reilly Radar, "The truth about data: Once it's out there, it's hard to control (*http://radar.oreilly.com/2011/04/jeff-jonas-data-privacy-control.html*)," April 4, 2011

23. Jessa Liying Wang & Michael C. Loui, University of Illinois at Urbana-Champaign, "Privacy and Ethical Issues in Location-Based Tracking Systems (*http://students.cse.unt.edu/~ry0049/lp3.pdf*)," 2009, pg. 1

24. Andy Miller, The Economist, "Untangling the Social Web," September 2, 2010

As shown in the preceding examples, it's clear that various government agencies have taken a page or two out of advertising's playbook, increasing their data collection efforts through collaboration with other agencies as well as third parties (commercial data collectors and markets), building large databases, and engaging in sophisticated data mining efforts. Some of these projects focus on operational efficiency (the Department of Veteran Affairs), others on fraud detection (Medicare and the IRS), criminal investigation (fusion centers), crime prevention, and counterterrorism. [26]

Certainly, various government agencies are intent on creating some very large databases:

- The FBI's Investigative Data Warehouse which houses operational and intelligence information from more than 53 data sources and holds, as of September 2008, nearly one billion documents.[27]

- The National Security Agency's secret collection of "… phone call records of tens of millions of Americans, using data provided by AT&T, Verizon, and Bell-South."[28]

- The Transportation Security Agency's possible resurrection of an airline passenger profiling system (similar to the now defunct and controversial Computer Aided Passenger Pre-Screening System (*http://www.aclu.org/technology-and-liberty/posi tive-profiling-problem-learning-us-experience*)) that would most likely rely on commercial data sources and PNRs (passenger travel records)[29] that reveal a great deal of personal information (*http://www.hasbrouck.org/articles/pnr.html*) about a passenger (flights, hotel and rental car reservations, meal preferences, emergency contacts, special room requests, notes about tastes and preferences, the list really does go on and on).

Much of the efforts are focused, of course, on pulling together information from multiple data sources:

> "The 2004 GAO report on government data mining found that more than one-fourth of all government data mining projects involved access to data from the private sector. The government has broad powers for doing so. It can access publicly available data on the same basis as any member of the public, it can contract for data, and it can exercise its

25. MacDaily News, "Police adopting iPhone-based facial-recognition device, raising civil-rights questions (*http://macdailynews.com/2011/07/13/police-adopting-iphone-based-facial-recognition-device-raising -civil-rights-questions/*)," July 13, 2011

26. The Constitution Project, "Principles for Government Data Mining: Preserving Civil Liberties in the Information Age, (*http://www.constitutionproject.org/pdf/dataminingpublication.pdf*)" 2010,m pg. 9

27. Electronic Frontier Foundation, "Report on the Investigative Data Warehouse (*http://www.eff.org/issues/ foia/investigative-data-warehouse-report*)," April 2009

28. Roger Wollenberg, USA Today, "NSA has massive database of Americans' phone calls (*http://www .usatoday.com/news/washington/2006-05-10-nsa_x.htm*)," May 11, 2006

29. Jay Stanley, Huff Post Politics, "Airline Passenger Profiling: Back from the Grave? (*http://www .huffingtonpost.com/jay-stanley/airline-passenger-profili_b_820476.htmll*)," February 8, 2011

unique power to issue subpoenas, search warrants, wiretap orders, National Security Letters, and FISA orders that require the product of personal data, usually in secret."[30]

It's clear that federal agencies are increasingly delving into "... the vast commercial market for consumer information, such as buying habits and financial records, ... tapping into data that would be difficult for the government to accumulate but that has become a booming business for private companies."[31]

However you may choose to characterize the U.S. privacy regulatory landscape, some effort has been, and is being, made to regulate privacy as it applies to the commercial sector. But our various government agencies are not held to those same regulatory standards as first shown by Miller v. United States:

> "In Miller v. United States and subsequent cases, the Supreme Court created a broad gap in the privacy protection provided by the Fourth Amendment by finding that the government's seizure of personal information from third parties is outside its scope. As a result, the government's behavior need not be reasonable nor is any judicial authorization required when the government searches or seizes personal information held by third parties."[32]

Privacy advocates or not, all of us should be troubled by the lack of privacy protections afforded us by government agencies. They are the beneficiaries of large troves of valuable personal information and yet, are not subject to any regulations regarding the usage of it. How do we ensure that the regulators are in fact, subject to the same privacy policies and laws?

Once we give out personal information, it is out of our control; it can be collected, stored, sold, rented, used, and analyzed for any number of purposes. If we don't know what will happen to our data as it passes through any number of hands, than how can we make any decision about what to give away and what to keep? Do we assume, as Danah Boyd recommended (see Chapter 2), that our online behavior is public by default and private by effort? Do we rely upon privacy watchdog groups, consumers, and the various regulatory agencies to monitor and identify the most egregious privacy violations to keep the collectors, markets, and applications providers (and users) honest? Do we lobby our legislature for more comprehensive privacy policies that apply to all government agencies? Some argue that privacy, as we knew it, no longer exists. But, throughout history (ours and the rest of the world's), someone has always argued that very point. Perhaps we should say instead, that privacy must be redefined within the framework of our digital world.

---

30. Newton N. Minow, Fred H. Cate, McGraw Hill Handbook of Homeland Security, "Government Data Mining (*http://papers.ssrn.com/sol3/papers.cfm?abstract_id=1156989&*)," July 8, 2008, pg. 21

31. Ashad Mohammed and Sara Kehaulani Goo, The Washington Post, "Government Increasingly Turning to Data Mining (*http://www.washingtonpost.com/wp-dyn/content/article/2006/06/14/ar2006061402063.html*)," June 15, 2006

32. Fred H. Cate, Harvard Civil Rights-Civil Liberties Law Review, "Government Data Mining: The Need for a Legal Framework (*http://www.law.harvard.edu/students/orgs/crcl/vol43_2/435-490_cate.pdf*)," Vol. 43, May 21, 2008, pg. 485

Those that Protect and Serve in the Name of Privacy

While U.S. companies and various government agencies (ours and others around the world) are some of the largest collectors of personal information in the world, there are no comprehensive U.S. privacy regulations. Most privacy actions are handled in state courts via tort law where actual harm must be shown unlike the EU and other regions that have comprehensive privacy regulations and a very different view of privacy. As a result, much of U.S. privacy policing is accomplished through watchdog organizations, regulatory agencies (see Chapter 3), and industry self-regulatory agencies. And of course, blogs and the media can often be counted on to discover and report issues and violations.

There are a number of privacy organizations, like the Electronic Privacy Information Center (*http://epic.org/*) (EPIC), American Civil Liberties Union (*http://www.aclu.org/*) (ALCU), and Electronic Frontier Foundation (*http://www.eff.org/*). These organizations cover privacy policy as it applies to children, smartphones, the government, social networks, and a host of others. They institute and/or cover legal privacy-related court cases, provide research and analysis, and give guidance on how to prevent privacy violations. For a comprehensive list of U.S. and international organizations and what they cover, go to EPIC's (*http://epic.org/privacy/privacy_resources_faq.html*)[33] online guide to privacy resources.

There are alliances and organizations, largely promoted by the advertising industry and data collectors in a bid to prevent more privacy legislation, which provide regulation guidelines and certify those companies that adhere to them. A coalition of trade groups recently announced the Digital Advertising Alliance (*http://adage.com/article/digital/advertisers-adopt-stricter-codes-digital-privacy/228025/*), a program designed to self-regulate digital tracking practices and offer consumers who do not wish to be tracked an opt out icon. Participating companies include major advertisers, like AT&T, Verizon, Dell, and Bank of America, and major ad networks, like AOL, Google, Microsoft, and Yahoo. However, according to ComScore, of the top 200 advertisers, 181 are not taking part in this program.

The Network Advertising Alliance (*http://www.networkadvertising.org/index.asp*) is an association of advertising networks, data exchanges, and marketing analytics services providers. It educates consumers on how they can protect themselves online, provides information on what is being tracked, and offers consumers a way to opt out (*http://www.networkadvertising.org/managing/opt_out.asp*) of participating members behavioral advertising programs. There is also a Self-Regulatory Program for Online Behavioral Targeting (*http://www.aboutads.info/*), launched by some of the largest media and marketing associations (that represent (*http://arstechnica.com/web/news/2010/10/opting-out-of-behavioral-ad-tracking-may-get-easier.ars*) more than 5,000 companies that

---

33. URL: *http://epic.org/privacy/privacy_resources_faq.html*

advertise on the web). It features an Advertising Option Icon that alerts consumers if the site is engaged in behavioral advertising and offers an easy opt out.

As with any other part of the privacy landscape, the number of organizations that monitor various aspects of privacy as it applies to industries, topics, or issues, is vast. The cynics among us (and we are a part of this group) might be asking this question: if much of privacy enforcement happens after a violation, how many violations go unreported? In other words, how do we protect ourselves if we don't know what we're protecting ourselves from? Whenever there is a vacuum, something rushes to fill it up as evidenced by the number of companies offering consumers' privacy solutions and providing businesses and organizations ways to certify that they meet privacy guidelines in the U.S. and abroad.

The Rising Privacy Economy

While the erosion of privacy may be big business, there are all kinds of companies rising to a different challenge: preserving, or often redefining, consumer privacy to better fit the digital framework in which we live. There are companies that help businesses and organizations certify they meet specific privacy standards. There are companies and a host of tools that help consumers block tracking and monitoring. There are companies that help consumers control their personal data in a number of new and interesting ways and there are movements intent on recasting privacy in the digital age.

Over the years, studies have shown that consumers are becoming more concerned about Internet privacy but, as a recent Harris Interactive Poll highlights, they are now also assuming responsibility for it: 92 percent indicating that they have some responsibility for protecting their data, a majority expecting organizations to assume responsibility, and 42 percent indicating that they trust themselves most to protect their privacy.[34] They are also willing to pay for it. Recent research from Carnegie Mellon University indicates that privacy may very well be a key competitive advantage for companies in the digital age:

> "Our results offer new insight into consumers' valuations of personal data and provide evidence that privacy information affects online shopping decision making. We found that participants provided with salient privacy information took that information into consideration making purchases from websites offering medium or high levels of privacy. Our results indicate that, contrary to the common view that consumers are unlikely to pay for privacy, consumers may be willing to pay a premium for privacy. Our results also indicate that business may use technological means to showcase their privacy-friendly privacy policies and thereby gain a competitive advantage."[35]

---

34. New TRUSTe Survey Finds (*http://www.admonsters.com/article/new-truste-survey-finds-consumer-education-and-transparency-vital-sustainable-growth-and-suc*) Consumer Education and Transparency Vital for Sustainable Growth and Success of Online Behavioral Advertising, July 25, 2011

The success of online privacy solutions providers, such as TRUSTe (*http://www.truste .com/about_truste/index.html*), who has certified over 4,000 web properties, as well as the advertising industries focus on offering consumers tracking opt outs and more **transparency** on what is being tracked, certainly attest to an increasing focus on privacy from both a business and consumer perspective. Companies, like Google (via its Me on the Web (*http://thenextweb.com/google/2011/06/15/google-releases-me-on-the -web-tool-to-help-monitor-your-web-identity/*) and Ad Preferences (*http://www.google .com/ads/preferences/view?sig=aci0tchwjzdxt-c3hanaah9xug0zitgkuq6mhtv3a -zp0kyy3uq6cw7y5vom2buwu7rf70stoiqwx9zhygzgi1tgdcvsmduima&hl=en*) tools) and RapLeaf (via its See Your Info (*https://www.rapleaf.com/people/see_your_info*) page), are also providing information on what is being tracked as well as offering consumers the ability to edit information or opt out.

For savvy users, there are a host of tools available (*http://epic.org/privacy/tools.html*) that block cookies, ensure email and file privacy, enable anonymous surfing, etc. For most, however, the sheer number of tools that may be employed for various aspects of privacy is daunting. But, just like antivirus software, it is likely that there will be privacy versions that combine these tools (or something like them) into one easy solution.

There are also new privacy business models (*http://www.mercurynews.com/business/ci _18349132?source=rss*) that allow consumers to find out what information is available about them, repair false information, and even determine what information they wish to share with advertisers. MyPrivacy (*http://www.reputation.com/myprivacy*) removes personal information from websites. MyReputation (*http://www.reputation.com/myre putation*) monitors your online presence and customizes it to present you or your business in the best possible light. SafetyWeb (*http://www.safetyweb.com/*) protects your child's online reputation and privacy. Singly (*http://singly.com/*) allows people to aggregate and own their personal data through digital lockers (*http://blogs.forbes.com/ smcnally/2011/06/30/your-digital-wake/*).

Privacy by Design (PbD), (*http://www.ipc.on.ca/images/resources/7foundationalprinci ples.pdf*) a framework for building privacy into products or services developed by Ann Cavoukian, Canada's Information and Privacy Commissioner, is taking center stage as it forms the basis of the FTC's proposed framework (*http://www.ftc.gov/os/2010/12/ 101201privacyreport.pdf*) for businesses and policymakers. There is also a Silicon Valley trade group, the Personal Data Ecosystem Consortium (*http://personaldataecosys tem.org/*) which promotes and supports the idea that individual control their own data through the use of personal data stores and services as well as organizations, like the International Association of Privacy Professionals (*https://www.privacyassociation .org/*) (iapp), focused on developing and supporting privacy professionals throughout the world.

---

35. Janice Y. Tsai, Serge Egelman, Lorrie Cranor, Alessandro Acquisti, Information Systems Research, "The Effect of Online Privacy Information on Purchasing Behavior: An Experimental Study (*http:// isr.journal.informs.org/cgi/content/abstract/22/2/254*)," Vol. 22, No. 2, June 2011, pp. 266

There are many pundits who argue that privacy is dead but the desire for privacy certainly is not. While the emerging privacy ecosystem can help consumers regain some control over their personal information, they must do so within a digital framework. One way or another, a new era of privacy is upon us.

While the Players are Playing, Consumer Privacy Continues to Erode

Our personal information is used to feed all kinds of business models. In fact, we are the fuel for what has become a multi-billion dollar economic engine. And once the data leaves collectors' hands, we, the consumers, have absolutely no control over who uses it or for what purpose. Technology marches on—in the form of big data storage, access, and analytics, new and improved devices, embedded TPM chips, RFID tags on everything, the smart grid (*http://en.wikipedia.org/wiki/smart_grid*)—and has made it possible to figure out who we are from three easily attained pieces of data: birth date, gender, and zip code. So where does this leave us?

Well, we've allowed our data to be collected in return for services that we value and the devices that we use. Perhaps we should ask ourselves this question again: how much privacy are we willing to give up for our online services and devices? If your answer is all of it, continue doing what you're doing. If you find yourself wondering if this may be too high a price to pay, we don't have any easy answers for you.

There's an old saying: you can't unring the bell (*http://www.usingenglish.com/reference/idioms/you+can't+unring+a+bell.html*). The data that we all put out there, knowingly or not, is out there. You cannot take it back. It travels through lots of hands, and is traded and copied. Although the EU is proposing a new law (*http://www.telegraph.co.uk/technology/internet/8388033/online-right-to-be-forgotten-confirmed-by-eu.html*), the right to be forgotten (where websites may be compelled to delete all the data it has for a specific user), here is the unvarnished truth: that same information is most likely housed in databases all over the world. You will never be able to erase it.

So what can you do? Well, you can be more conscious of what you do online and understand that pretty much everything out there is public information and is for all practical purposes immortal. You can cull down the number of sites you belong to, put up fewer photos and videos, and understand that when you search for something it's being tracked. You can use various tools to prevent tracking as well as monitor and ensure the security of your devices from malware. You can monitor the privacy websites and engage with your legislators on what can be done in terms of privacy regulations and policies.

But if you, like us, live in the industrialized world and desire a convenient and full life, your online privacy future is bleak. You can't unring this bell, but you can reduce your exposure, keeping in mind that (similar to Las Vegas): "What happens on the Internet stays, on the Internet forever." Our advice: your best bet for a semblance of digital privacy is to control how much information you put out there, keep yourself informed about how privacy impacts the technologies you use, and vote with your dollars against companies that abuse your trust.

Bibliography

1. Peephal.com, "Privacy Leakage on Popular Web Sites (*http://peephal.com/privacy -leakage-on-popular-web-sites*)," June 17, 2011

2. Professor John Blackie, "The Doctrinal History of Privacy Protection in Unity and Complexity," University of Strathclyde

3. Gerard Alexander, "Illiberal Europe (*http://www.aei.org/doclib/20060623_otialex anderforposting_g.pdf*)," American Institute for Public Policy Research, 2006

4. Jacob Mchangama, National Review Online, "Censorship as Tolerance (*http:// www.nationalreview.com/articles/243451/censorship-tolerance-jacob-mchan gama*)," July 19, 2010

5. Benjamin D. Brunk, First Monday: Peer-Reviewed Journal on the Internet, "Understanding the Privacy Space (*http://firstmonday.org/htbin/cgiwrap/bin/ojs/index .php/fm/article/view/991/912*)," Volume 7, Number 10, October 2002

6. Joseph Turow, Lauren Feldman, & Kimberly Meltzer, Annenberg Public Policy Center, "Open to Exploitation: American Shoppers Online and Offline (*http:// www.annenbergpublicpolicycenter.org/downloads/information_and_society/turow _appc_report_web_final.pdf*)," June 2005

7. Janice Y. Tsai, Serge Egelman, Lorrie Cranor, Alessandro Acquisti, Information Systems Research, "The Effect of Online Privacy Information on Purchasing Behavior: An Experimental Study (*http://isr.journal.informs.org/cgi/content/abstract/ 22/2/254*)," Vol. 22, No. 2, June 2011, pp. 254-268

8. David S. Evans, University College London and University of Chicago, "The Online Advertising Industry: Economics, Evolution, and Privacy," April 2009

9. Kenneth C. Laudon & Jane Price Laudon, Management Information Systems: Managing the Digital Firm, "Chapter 4: Ethical and Social Issues in Information Systems (*http://www.prenhall.com/behindthebook/0132304619/*)," April 2005

10. Nate Anderson, arsTechnica, "U.S. Government finally admits most piracy estimates are bogus," August 2010

11. GAO Report to Congressional Committees, "Intellectual Property: Observations on Efforts to Quantify the Economic Effects of Counterfeit and Pirated Goods," April 2010

12. Ross Anderson, "Trusted Computing Frequently Asked Questions (*http://en.wiki pedia.org/wiki/european_union_copyright_directive*)," August 2003

13. Paul Boutin, Salon, "U.S. prepares to invade your hard drive (*http://www.salon .com/technology/feature/2002/03/29/hollings_bill/*)," March 29, 2002

14. Tomas Claburn, InformationWeek, "Amazon Says It Will Stop Deleting Kindle Books (*http://www.informationweek.com/news/personal-tech/digital-content/218501227*)," July 17,2009

15. Testimony and Statement (*http://epic.org/privacy/copyright/epic-wipo-testimony-698.html*) for the Record of Marc Rotenberg, Director, Electronic Privacy Information Center Adjunct Professor, Georgetown University Law Center Senior Lecturer, Washington College of Law, on H.R. 2281. The WIPO Copyright Treaties Implementation Act and Privacy Issues, Before the Subcommittee on Telecommunications, Trade, and Consumer Protection, Committee on Commerce, U.S. House of Representatives, June 5, 1998

16. Jim Finkle, msnbc.com, "Biggest-ever series of cyber attacks uncovered, UN hit (*http://www.msnbc.msn.com/id/43998147/ns/technology_and_science-security/#.tjlblyixg4q*)," August 3, 2011

17. Cecilia Kang, The Washington Post, "Web firms face increased federal scrutiny over Internet privacy (*http://www.washingtonpost.com/business/economy/web-firms-face-increased-federal-scrutiny-over-internet-privacy/2011/04/06/afvrep1c_story.html*)," April 8, 2011

18. Julia Angwin, Wall Street Journal, "The Web's New Gold Mine: Your Secrets (*http://online.wsj.com/article/sb10001424052748703940904575395073512989404.html?mod=what_they_know*)," July 30, 2010

19. Julia Angwin, Wall Street Journal, "Latest in Web Tracking: Stealthy Supercookies," August 18, 2011

20. Geoffrey A. Fowler, Wall Street Journal, "More Questions for Wall Street (*http://online.wsj.com/article/sb10001424052702304410504575560640816473962.html?mod=wsj_hpp_middletopstories*)," October 18, 2010

21. David Goldman, CNNMoney, "Rapleaf is selling your identity (*http://money.cnn.com/2010/10/21/technology/rapleaf/index.htm*)," October 21, 2010

22. Balanchander Krishnamurthy, Konstatin Naryshkin, Craig E. Wills, AT&T Labs and Worcester Polytechnic Institute, "Privacy leakage vs. Protection measures: the growing disconnect (*http://w2spconf.com/2011/papers/privacyvsprotection.pdf*)," 2011

23. Balanchander Krishnamurthy, Craig E. Wills, ACM SIGCOMM Computer Communication Review "On the Leakage of Personally Identifiable Information Via Online Social Networks (*http://portal.acm.org/citation.cfm?id=1672328*)," 2010

24. Emily Steel, Wall Street Journal, "WPP Ad Unit Has Your Profile (*http://online.wsj.com/article/sb10001424052702304444780457640956292285 9314.html#ixzz1qhf7phes*)," June 27, 2011

25. Jenn Webb, O'Reilly Radar, "The truth about data: Once it's out there, it's hard to control (*http://radar.oreilly.com/2011/04/jeff-jonas-data-privacy-control.html*)," April 4, 2011

26. Jessa Liying Wang & Michael C. Loui, University of Illinois at Urbana-Champaign, "Privacy and Ethical Issues in Location-Based Tracking Systems (*http://students.cse.unt.edu/~ry0049/lp3.pdf*)," 2009

27. ALgorithm Adaptation, Dissemenation and IntegrationN Center, Privacy in Data Workshop (*http://www.aladdin.cs.cmu.edu/workshops/privacy/index.html*), March 2003

28. New TRUSTe Survey Finds (*http://www.admonsters.com/article/new-truste-survey-finds-consumer-education-and-transparency-vital-sustainable-growth-and-suc*) Consumer Education and Transparency Vital for Sustainable Growth and Success of Online Behavioral Advertising, July 25, 2011

29. Janice Y. Tsai, Serge Egelman, Lorrie Cranor, Alessandro Acquisti, Information Systems Research, "The Effect of Online Privacy Information on Purchasing Behavior: An Experimental Study (*http://isr.journal.informs.org/cgi/content/abstract/22/2/254*)," Vol. 22, No. 2, June 2011

30. Peter K. Yu, "Digital Copyright and Confuzzling Rhetoric (*http://www.scribd.com/doc/53965731/digital-copyright-and-con-fuzz-ling-rhetoric*)," April 27, 2011

31. Ville Okansen, Mikko Valimaki, International Journal of Media Management, "Transnational Advocacy Network Opposing DRM (*http://www.mediajournal.org/ojs/index.php/jmm/article/viewfile/225/112*) – a Technical and Legal Challenge to Media Companies," 2002

32. Marc Rotenberg, Stanford Technology Law Review, "Fair Information Practices and the Architecture of Privacy (*http://stlr.stanford.edu/2001/02/fair-information-practices-and-the-architecture-of-privacy/*) (What Larry Doesn't Get), 2001

33. R. Anthony Reese, Columbia Journal of Law and the Arts, "Innocent Infringement in U.S. Copyright Law: A History (*http://papers.ssrn.com/sol3/papers.cfm?abstract_id=1153602*)," Vol. 30, No. 2, 2007

34. Pamela Samuelson, "Privacy As Intellectual Property? (*http://www.jstor.org/pss/1229511*)," 2000

35. Alberto Cerda Silva, American University Washington College of Law, "**Enforcing Intellectual Property Rights by Diminishing Privacy: How the Anti-Counterfeiting Trade Agreement Jeopardizes the Right to Privacy**," September 1, 2010

36. Mika D. Ayenson, Dietrich J. Wambach, Ashkan Soltani, Nathaniel Good, & Jay Hoofnagle, "Flash Cookies and Privacy II: Now with HTML5 and ETag Respawning (*http://www.techpolicy.com/flashcookiesprivacyii.aspx*)," August 1, 2011

37. Burst Media, Online Insights, "Online Privacy Still a Consumer Concern (*http://www.burstmedia.com/pdfs/research/2009_02_01.pdf*)," February 2009

38. Burst Media, Online Insights, "Behavioral Targeting, Privacy, and the Impact on Online Advertising, (*http://www.burstmedia.com/pdfs/research/burst_media_online_insights_12_10_2010.pdf*)" December 2010

39. Joseph Turow, Lauren Feldman, & Kimberly Meltzer, Annenberg Policy Center, "Open to Exploitation: American Shoppers Online and Offline, (*http://www.an nenbergpublicpolicycenter.org/newsdetails.aspx?myid=31*)" June 1, 2005

40. Mary DeRosa, Center for Strategic and International Studies (CSIS), "Data Mining and Data Analysis for Counterterrorism (*http://csis.org/files/media/csis/pubs/ 040301_data_mining_report.pdf*)," March 2004

41. David S. Evans, Journal of Economic Perspectives, "The Online Advertising Industry: Economics, Evolution, and Privacy (*http://www.intertic.org/policy%20pa pers/evanseoai.pdf*)," April 2009

42. The Constitution Project, "Principles for Government Data Mining: Preserving Civil Liberties in the Information Age, (*http://www.constitutionproject.org/pdf/da taminingpublication.pdf*)" 2010

43. Andy Miller, The Economist, "**Untangling the Social Web**," September 2, 2010

44. MacDaily News, "Police adopting iPhone-based facial-recognition device, raising civil-rights questions (*http://macdailynews.com/2011/07/13/police-adopting -iphone-based-facial-recognition-device-raising-civil-rights-questions/*)," July 13, 2011

45. Electronic Frontier Foundation, "Report on the Investigative Data Warehouse (*http://www.eff.org/issues/foia/investigative-data-warehouse-report*)," April 2009

46. Roger Wollenberg, USA Today, "NSA has massive database of Americans' phone calls (*http://www.usatoday.com/news/washington/2006-05-10-nsa_x.htm*)," May 11, 2006

47. Ellen Nakashima, Washington Post, "FBI Shows off Counterterrorism Database (*http://www.washingtonpost.com/wp-dyn/content/article/2006/08/29/ ar2006082901520.html*)," August 30, 2006

48. American Civil Liberties Union, "The Positive Profiling Problem: Learning from the U.S. Experience (*http://www.aclu.org/technology-and-liberty/positive-profiling -problem-learning-us-experience*)," October 1, 2006

49. Edward Hasbrouck, The Practical Nomad, "What's in a Passenger Name Record (PNR)? (*http://www.hasbrouck.org/articles/pnr.html*)"

50. Jay Stanley, Huff Post Politics, "Airline Passenger Profiling: Back from the Grave? (*http://www.huffingtonpost.com/jay-stanley/airline-passenger-profili_b _820476.htmll*)," February 8, 2011

51. United States General Accounting Office, "Data Mining: Federal Efforts Cover a Wide Range of Uses (*http://www.gao.gov/new.items/d04548.pdf*)," May 2004

52. Newton N. Minow, Fred H. Cate, McGraw Hill Handbook of Homeland Security, "Government Data Mining (*http://papers.ssrn.com/sol3/papers.cfm?abstract_id= 1156989&*)," July 8, 2008, pg. 21

53. Ashad Mohammed and Sara Kehaulani Goo, The Washington Post, "Government Increasingly Turning to Data Mining (*http://www.washingtonpost.com/wp-dyn/content/article/2006/06/14/ar2006061402063.html*)," June 15, 2006

54. Fred H.Cate, Harvard Civil Rights-Civil Liberties Law Review, "Government Data Mining: The Need for a Legal Framework (*http://www.law.harvard.edu/students/orgs/crcl/vol43_2/435-490_cate.pdf*)," Vol. 43, May 21, 2008

CHAPTER 5

Making Sense of It All

"Like it or not, we live in interesting times."[1] Coined by Robert Kennedy in a graduation speech to the National Union of South African Students in 1966 (with some argument as to whether its origins lie in a Chinese curse or proverb (*http://en.wikipedia.org/wiki/may_you_live_in_interesting_times*)), Kennedy was alluding to the ongoing Civil Rights movement:

> "Like it or not, we live in interesting times. They are times of danger and uncertainty; but they are also the most creative of any time in the history of mankind. And everyone here will ultimately be judged -- will ultimately judge himself -- on the effort he has contributed to building a new world society and the extent to which his ideals and goals have shaped that effort."[2]

Every generation faces seminal moments in history where a path must be taken and that path will shape the future. There are always inflection points where the unknown becomes known. There are always moments when the actions we take have unintended consequences; how we deal with those consequences will define us as individuals, businesses, governments, and countries.

The Internet is a powerful, disruptive force. It has altered the world in fundamental ways, creating waves of change across the economic, social and political landscape. The collection of so much personally identifiable information via our laptops, iPods, Smartphones, and the Internet of Things has been combined with cheap and accessible big data technology that can capture, analyze, and make predictions based on the digital trails we leave. The end result is all seeing and all knowing, which can be illuminating or frightening, depending on your perspective.

E-commerce and e-governance are commonplace. Our digital interactions are captured in real time, revealing things about us that we may not even know and predicting what

---

1. Robert F. Kennedy, Day of Affirmation Speech (*http://allthingsd.com/20110818/reid-hoffman-talks -linkedin-life-as-a-vc-and-gives-five-tips-to-start-ups/?mod=tweet*), June 6, 1966

2. Robert F. Kennedy, Day of Affirmation Address (*http://www.jfklibrary.org/research/ready-reference/ rfk-speeches/day-of-affirmation-address-news-release-text-version.aspx*), June 16, 1966

we will do next—before we ourselves even think about it. Like all powerful technology innovations, it is a double edged sword. It helped to enable the "Arab Spring (*http://en .wikipedia.org/wiki/arab_spring*)," inspiring the hopes of millions for greater democracy across the Middle East. At the same time, it has made it easy to automatically identify and monitor individuals or groups, discouraging dissent and other forms of political activism around the world.

In the digital world we now inhabit, is privacy outmoded or even possible? Should we just get over it and move on? Should we embrace transparency and its many benefits and disadvantages? And if we do, or have it forced upon us, can we expect the same from our governments, our corporations, and powerful individuals? Will they be held to the same standard? If not, since information is power, what will our world look like?

We seem to be caught in a tug-of-war between all kinds of players who come at privacy from different perspectives, ranging from the utopian to Orwellian views of big data's impact on privacy. There are those who would like us to cede all expectations of digital privacy – to live lives in a global public square, or a virtual Cheers (*http://www.cheer sboston.com/pub/*) "where everybody (everywhere) knows your name" as well as your salary and the ages of your kids. They argue that an open world breeds efficiency and safety; a society where services are delivered to us before we need them, corrupt politicians are outed on YouTube, and criminals are apprehended before any damage is done.

There are those who see the digital age (and the big data technologies that enable it) in stark Orwellian terms. They see it as a direct route to a tyrannical surveillance society where governments and corporations control what we read and write and where people's digital profiles are used to make pre-emptive arrests. They remind us of Hitler and Stalin, asking what will the next monster that rises amongst us do with big data as a platform?

There are those who lie somewhere in the middle, redefining what privacy means, and then seeking ways to protect it through regulations, frameworks, and business models. With such divergent views, is it any wonder that most conversations about privacy devolve into one side versus another, where much shouting is heard but very little is actually said or done, all while our technical capabilities continue to outpace our social structures.

The Heart of the Matter: Commodity Versus Right

What privacy means to each one of us is formed by our unique life experiences and informed by our culture, society, politics, religion, race, gender—it is our worldview. But at its core it revolves around these two questions:

- Is privacy a commodity that can be bought and sold?
- Or is privacy a basic human right that transcends commoditization?

As we look across the world, it is easy to see how countries align along one of these two paths. In the U.S., historically, privacy is a commodity. It is an asset, regulated by the courts via tort laws, and viewed as a second class citizen when framed against what we regard as our essential freedoms. When we consider an invasion of privacy, we first ask what is the harm? And, unlike the European view, that harm must be tangible.

For Europeans and other countries and regions, privacy is a basic human right that is equivalent to other freedoms. It is amorphous, viewed through a prism of respect and dignity. When they consider an invasion of privacy, they first ask how it harmed the individual. But to them, the harm is intangible, based on whether one might view this information as embarrassing or humiliating.

For repressive regimes across the world, it can be argued that privacy for ones citizenry does not exist. Information is censored as is speech as is the press. In this case, privacy is constantly violated to root out those dissidents that are viewed as "enemies of the state."

Of course, these views of privacy existed long before the digital age. Their roots can be traced back through the centuries. What is different about the world today is how interconnected we all are: the impact of what one does half way around the world can be felt by all of us.

We Are All Connected

In the digital age, there are no geographical borders. And yet, most governments have attempted to put restrictions on how their citizens' data are used.

In the U.S., privacy regulations follow the sectoral model; it governs specific items, like children's, medical, or financial privacy, with some self-regulation and consumer regulation thrown into the mix. When it comes to privacy, the U.S. is often characterized as one of the major perpetrators to its worldwide erosion. Certainly, Internet advertising began in the U.S. and started a domino effect in how personal data was collected and used. Equally, the big data and analytics technology that made the use of that data financially feasible and enabled easy linkage between multiple data sources (often removing assumed anonymity in the process), can also be traced back to the U.S. Then there are the most aggressive IP stakeholders, unleashing advanced DRM technology that has set in motion privacy's version of collateral damage. But make no mistake, governments and businesses around the world have embraced these U.S. "breakthroughs" and applied them for their own ends.

Although the U.S. may be late to the idea of a comprehensive digital privacy policy, we are seeing some enlightened individuals in the Senate and House of Representative introduce bills that would seek to restrict what is tracked and provide consumers with more information. Some of the more notable bills include:

- The Do Not Track Me Online Act of 2011 (*http://www.gpo.gov/fdsys/pkg/bills-112hr654ih/pdf/bills-112hr654ih.pdf*) which would essentially give consumers the right to opt out of online tracking.
- The Financial Information Privacy Act of 2011 (*http://www.gpo.gov/fdsys/pkg/bills-112hr653ih/pdf/bills-112hr653ih.pdf*) which would require opt-in consent by consumers before financial institutions could share their information with third parties.
- The Commercial Privacy Bill of Rights Act of 2011 (*http://kerry.senate.gov/imo/media/doc/commercial%20privacy%20bill%20of%20rights%20text.pdf*) that attempts to "strike a balance between protecting consumers from unauthorized tracking and allowing firms the flexibility to offer new services and technologies. Under the bill, companies must clearly communicate how they gather and use personal information while giving consumers the ability to opt out of any information collection unauthorized by the law."[3]
- The Data Accountability and Trust Act (*http://www.gpo.gov/fdsys/pkg/bills-112hr1707ih/pdf/bills-112hr1707ih.pdf*) which requires companies to establish policies on the collection, storage, sale, and retention of consumer's personal information and establishes a 60-day breach notification requirement.

In addition, the FTC has introduced a Privacy Framework (*http://www.ftc.gov/os/2010/12/101201privacyreport.pdf*) which supports the implementation of Privacy by Design (*http://privacybydesign.ca/about/*) (PbD), a concept developed by Ann Cavoukian, Ontario, Canada's Information and Privacy Commissioner, where privacy is embedded into technology itself. The Framework also includes simplified consumer choices where standard uses for data that is collected would not require prior consent, but anything else would require the consumer to opt-in, as well as greater transparency on the part of standardized privacy policies, consumer education, and more stringent policies regarding consumer notice and consent over any material changes. If this Framework were adopted, it would bring the U.S. closer to the EU model of a comprehensive privacy policy.

In addition to the state sponsored approaches there are many private organizations who have introduced various codes of conduct, such as the Privacy Bill of Rights and PbD. These organizations recognize technology advances well before the regulatory environment does. Their approach of working with companies to design privacy into solutions, websites, ecommerce, etc., can help to avoid the more egregious privacy violations. And at least some big businesses appear to be listening (*http://www.forbes.com/sites/kashmirhill/2011/07/28/why-privacy-by-design-is-the-new-corporate-hotness/*):

- Google+ was designed with privacy as a fundamental building block through its uses of non-public circles.

---

3. Gautham Nagesh, Hillicon Valley, **"Kerry and McCain throw their weight behind privacy bill of rights,"** April, 12, 2011

- Apple's iPhone now has a purple icon arrow that appears whenever your location is being sent to an application.
- GMAT no longer uses fingerprints to confirm test-takers' identities due to concerns about those fingerprints being "cross-purposed for criminal databases... GMAT switched to scans of palm veins."[4]

While we appreciate the genuine efforts of privacy advocates in government and across the world to protect digital privacy, we simply don't believe that laws or voluntary agreements can keep up with the pace of technology. Nor will it dissuade companies engaged in data collection due to the immense economic incentives that comes with it. But even if both of those issues were addressed, there would be no realistic global way to enforce laws or other types of policies. Certainly, the inability of the music and film industries to stop piracy serves as ample evidence that regulating the flow of data on the Internet is doomed to fail. Our point is this: as long as data is collected, it can be used in unexpected and even harmful ways and no law, policy, or framework in any state, country, or region can change that fact.

What Are We Willing to Give Up for Safety and Security?

As we've noted previously, when privacy is considered within the context of security and safety, it often comes out the loser. We have seen this happen in the U.S. and across the world which brings us back to this question: who regulates the regulators?

This is a legitimate question, as most of the regulatory and legislative actions we have looked at focus on the commercial uses of personal data. But governments are large collectors and users of data and are, for the most part, famously secretive about how they are using it. They are also quite capable of overlooking issues of privacy when dealing with issues of safety.

Certainly, the number of anti-terrorism laws on the books of most nations indicates a shift away from privacy, in favor of safety and security. From the U.S. PATRIOT Act (*http://en.wikipedia.org/wiki/usa_patriot_act*), to France's 2005 anti-terrorist law (*http://www.forbes.com/feeds/afx/2005/12/22/afx2410169.html*), to the U.K.'s Counter-Terrorism Act of 2008 (*http://www.ehow.com/facts_6770131_counter-terrorism-act-2008.html*), to Canada's Anti-Terrorism Act of 2001 (*http://en.wikipedia.org/wiki/canadian_anti-terrorism_act*), all give law enforcement and the government far more latitude to invade our privacy in order to keep us safe.

The Internet itself, or any digital device for that matter, is no longer exempt from the government's reach. For example, the U.K (*http://www.guardian.co.uk/uk/2011/aug/16/police-accessed-blackberry-messages-thwart-riots*)., under the Regulatory Investigatory Powers Act (RIPA), got access to the cell phone records of suspects in the recent

---

4. Kashmir Hill, Forbes, "Why Privacy by Design is the New Corporate Hotness (*http://www.forbes.com/sites/kashmirhill/2011/07/28/why-privacy-by-design-is-the-new-corporate-hotness/*)," July 28, 2011

London Riots. From that information, it was able to monitor Blackberry Messenger (BBM) and Twitter in real-time to prevent planned attacks at some of the most know London landmarks. The police also considered turning off social messaging sites but were told that the legality of doing so was questionable.[5] More ominous for the future:

> "In the wake of the riots in London, the *British government says it's considering shutting down access to social networks* (http://www.guardian.co.uk/media/2011/aug/11/david-cameron-rioters-social-media) — as well as Research In Motion's BlackBerry messenger service — and is asking the companies involved to help. *Prime Minister David Cameron said* (http://www.number10.gov.uk/news/pm-statement-on-disorder-in-england/) not only is his government considering banning individuals from social media if they are suspected of causing disorder, but it has asked Twitter and other providers to take down posts that are contributing to unrest."[6]

In San Francisco, the Bay Area Rapid Transit (Bart) commuter system shut down mobile phone service in some stations to prevent protesters from organizing a protest over a fatal shooting of a man by police at one of those stations.

It certainly appears that censorship is alive and well, not just in repressive regimes but in democracies too. (As we noted previously (*http://www.nytimes.com/2011/04/09/world/middleeast/09rights.html*), more than 40 countries restrict online access to some extent while more than 90 countries have laws that control organizations in order to monitor the communications of "someone" whether that someone is a political opponent, human rights activist, journalist, or labor organizer.) As we've illustrated throughout this book, law enforcement and government agencies are subject to few privacy regulations, and when they are, they work around those limits through loopholes such as the U.S. government's purchase or seizure of third party data, as they are not held to any protection of privacy for third party personal information.

The Truth About Data: Once It's Out There, It's Hard to Control

Over the decades, it has been shown again and again that our offline concept of privacy is very different from our online concept.[7] Consumer fears over loss of privacy have been steadily rising and unsurprisingly, are focused on the advertising industry. After all, they were the first to leverage technology and create a multi-billion dollar industry built on our personal data, and once it's out there, it is pretty hard to control.

Let's not forget the other, equally large, players riding on their coattails. Powerful groups, like the MPAA and RIAA and their international counterparts, have borrowed

---

5. Vikram Dodd, guardian.co.uk, "Police accessed Blackberry messages to thwart planned riots (*http://www.guardian.co.uk/uk/2011/aug/16/police-accessed-blackberry-messages-thwart-riots*)," August 16, 2011

6. Matthew Ingram, GIGAOM, "Blaming the tools: Britain proposes a social media ban (*http://gigaom.com/2011/08/11/blaming-the-tools-britain-proposes-a-social-media-ban/*)," August 11, 2011

7. Jenn Webb, O'Reilly Radar, "The truth about data: Once it's out there, it's hard to control (*http://radar.oreilly.com/2011/04/jeff-jonas-data-privacy-control.html*)," April 4, 2011

from advertising's playbook and extended it to every device we own. Today, it's not just about tracking our online behavior; it's about tracking what we do within the "four walls" of any device that we own and being able to remotely control them without our permission. These technologies and policies could end up delivering a mortal blow to privacy as well as cede to the government and IP holders unprecedented control over what media we are allowed to consume and share. However you look at this, it's a high price to pay to support an old business model that is unable to adapt to new technology.

At the same time, there are groups fighting to preserve privacy in the digital age, calling for more comprehensive privacy legislation and holding businesses and government agencies accountable when privacy violations are surfaced. There are businesses rising up to meet the privacy challenge, sometimes redefining it and sometimes offering consumers ways to mitigate the inherent lack of privacy that is the price we pay for living in a digital world.

Coming Full Circle

It seems that we are back where we started. Historically, as small tribes of hunter and gatherers we had no concept of privacy. Then, as we became rooted in towns and villages, we continued to live primarily in the public square where everyone "knew our business." With industrialization and the development of large dense urban areas, privacy was possible for the more privileged members of society and then, finally, for all of us.

We have come full circle. Again, we live our lives in a public, although now digital, square where any person, company, or organization around the world can watch us, whether we want them to or not. There is more known about us than ever before. What does privacy mean in the world we now live in?

This is not the first time (and certainly won't be the last) that technology has leapfrogged ethics, bringing us to the age old question of what we can do versus what we should do. The question we should all be asking ourselves, our communities, our societies, and our leaders is this: does privacy still matter in the digital age? Yes, privacy still matters in this age of big data and digital devices. But what it means, how we regulate and enforce it, what we are willing to give up for it, how much power we give our governments over it, remains to be seen.

Like it or not, we live in interesting times.

Bibliography

1. 112th Congress, 1st Session, H.R.654 (*http://www.gpo.gov/fdsys/pkg/bills -112hr654ih/pdf/bills-112hr654ih.pdf*), Do Not Track Me Online Act
2. 112th Congress, 1st Session, H.R.653 (*http://www.gpo.gov/fdsys/pkg/bills -112hr653ih/pdf/bills-112hr653ih.pdf*), Financial Privacy Information Act of 2011

3. Gautham Nagesh, Hillicon Valley, "**Kerry and McCain throw their weight behind privacy bill of rights**," April, 12, 2011

4. 112th Congress, 1st Session, S., Commercial Privacy Bill of Rights Act of 2011 (*http://kerry.senate.gov/imo/media/doc/commercial%20privacy%20bill%20of%20rights%20text.pdf*)

5. 112th Congress, 1st Session, H.R.1707, Data Accountability and Trust Act (*http://www.gpo.gov/fdsys/pkg/bills-112hr1707ih/pdf/bills-112hr1707ih.pdf*)

6. Tim Lisko, Privacy Wonk, "112th Privacy Legislation (*http://www.gpo.gov/fdsys/pkg/BILLS-112hr1707ih/pdf/bills-112hr1707ih.pdf*)," August 2, 2011

7. Preliminary FTC Staff Report, "Protecting Consumer Privacy in an Era of Rapid Change: A Proposed Framework for Businesses and Policymakers (*http://www.ftc.gov/os/2010/12/101201privacyreport.pdf*)," December 2010

8. IT Law Group, "ftc's privacy framework (*http://www.itlawgroup.com/resources/articles/189-ftcs-privacy-framework-similarities-with-eu-privacy-directives.html*): similarities with eu privacy directives," December 10, 2010

9. Kashmir Hill, Forbes, "Why Privacy by Design is the New Corporate Hotness (*http://www.forbes.com/sites/kashmirhill/2011/07/28/why-privacy-by-design-is-the-new-corporate-hotness/*)," July 28, 2011

10. Out-Law.com, "UK privacy laws are fundamentally flawed, report says (*http://www.out-law.com/default.aspx?page=12160&lang=en-gb&utm_source=feedburner&utm_medium=feed&utm_campaign=feed:+out-law-newsroundup+(out-law+news-roundup)&utm_content=google+reader*)," August 17, 2011

11. Charles Raab, Benjamin Goold, Equality and Human Rights Commission Research report 69, "Protecting information privacy (*http://www.equalityhumanrights.com/uploaded_files/research/rr69.pdf*)," Summer 2011

12. Vikram Dodd, guardian.co.uk, "Police accessed Blackberry messages to thwart planned riots (*http://www.guardian.co.uk/uk/2011/aug/16/police-accessed-blackberry-messages-thwart-riots*)," August 16, 2011

13. Matthew Ingram, GIGAOM, "Blaming the tools: Britain proposes a social media ban (*http://gigaom.com/2011/08/11/blaming-the-tools-britain-proposes-a-social-media-ban/*)," August 11, 2011

14. Reuters, guardian.co.uk, "Anonymous protests close San Francisco underground stations (*http://www.guardian.co.uk/world/2011/aug/16/anonymous-protests-san-francisco-bart*)," August 16, 2011

15. AFX News Limited, Forbes, "French parliament adopts tough anti-terrorism law (*http://www.forbes.com/feeds/afx/2005/12/22/afx2410169.html*)," December 12, 2005

16. Ned Millis, eHow, "The Counter Terrorism Act 2008 (*http://www.ehow.com/facts_6770131_counter-terrorism-act-2008.html*)," July 24, 2010

17. Wikipedia, "Canadian Anti-Terrorism Act (*http://en.wikipedia.org/wiki/canadian_anti-terrorism_act*)"

18. Wikipedia, "USA Patriot Act (*http://en.wikipedia.org/wiki/usa_patriot_act*)"

19. Steven Lee Myers, The New York Times, "Rights Abuses Extend Across Middle East, Report Says (*http://www.nytimes.com/2011/04/09/world/middleeast/09rights.html?_r=2*)," April 8, 2011

20. Jenn Webb, O'Reilly Radar, "The truth about data: Once it's out there, it's hard to control (*http://radar.oreilly.com/2011/04/jeff-jonas-data-privacy-control.html*)," April 4, 2011

21. Danah Boyd, Personal Democracy Forum 2011, "Networked Privacy (*http://www.danah.org/papers/talks/2011/pdf2011.html*)," June 6, 2011

Afterword

Over the course of writing this book we have been asked many times about how it was to collaborate on this grand production of ours. The next question, of course, was whether we changed our minds about the state of privacy in the age of big data. (And the final question was where we still friends? The answer, unequivocally, is yes.) Within the book, we tried to represent all sides of the privacy debate regardless of where we stood (although we are equally sure that you might be able to discern our opinions on some of the topics). This is our opportunity to share with you our thoughts (singularly as opposed to the all inclusive "we") on the process and on privacy in general.

Terence's Point of View

Mary and I have been friends and co-workers for a long time. This is our second startup together. It is considered a fait accompli in startup land that a technical founder/CEO (me) and a classically trained VP of Marketing (her), will not get along – but thankfully, in our case it has been a pleasant and fruitful collaboration with both of us learning from each other. So how hard could co-authoring a book (*http://oreilly.com/catalog/0636920020103*) be? Pretty damn hard, it turns out. There are the mechanics of the writing process itself, meeting deadlines, matching styles, fighting over different interpretations of grammar rules – Mary is a fan of Strunk & White (*http://en.wikipedia.org/wiki/strunk_%26_white*) and I, on the other hand, think e.e. cummings is a god. Then there is the content itself. Privacy, as we mention in the book, is one of "those topics" – as controversial in its way as what my Father called the bar fight trifecta: Religion, Politics and Another Man's Spouse. (Those three topics when combined with a couple of beers, could be guaranteed to get even the best of friends swinging bar stools at each other with abandon.)

Privacy seems to get people and governments just as riled up but with much broader consequences. For Mary and me, our virtual brawls always seemed to revolve around my adopting two seemingly incompatible positions – a fear of what the erosion of privacy by big data technology could mean and my agreement in the now known to be apocryphal quote by Mark Zuckerberg that "privacy is dead."

In my childhood, I was a U.S. citizen living in a country with a military dictatorship (Nigeria). I still remember with pride that after my Mom and I were evacuated with the rest of the U.S. women and children in the preamble and during the famously brutal Nigerian Civil War (*http://en.wikipedia.org/wiki/nigerian_civil_war*), many of the U.S citizens that remained, including my Father, hid university students and employees caught on the wrong side of the battle lines in their attics and basements.

The war resulted in over two million dead, many from starvation. If the refugees had been found, it is almost certain that both they, and the people giving them sanctuary, would have been killed out of hand. Having seen that tragedy unfold as well as having many close friends who suffered under the surveillance state that was the USSR, has always given me pause and helped to form my approach to digital privacy.

What if something like what happened in Nigeria happened here? In 2011, in any digitized nation, finding those refugees and the brave men that hid them would be simple. Using relatively cheap hardware and readily available commercial analytics software similar to the one sold by my company (*http://www.patternbuilders.com/*), finding them would have required nothing more than mashing up several easily available data sources: social media, cell phone transmissions, student, and employee records. Once likely supporters were "found," you could then correlate them with unusual deviances in power or water consumption or search loyalty card data for increased food or toilet paper purchases to discover their location.

Prior to writing this book, my approach to digital privacy was geared towards keeping as much information off the net as possible and, failing that, to keep it as inaccurate as possible. This struck many of my nearest and dearest as excessive and paranoid. I replied that until they had lived in a country that had been struck by war and understood how quickly things can unravel they would probably never understand. Writing the book changed my view in a couple of interesting ways.

The first is an admittedly defeatist one. I have come to believe that unless you are willing to live completely off the grid with all the inconvenience that it entails, you simply can't reasonably expect to maintain traditional levels of privacy from your neighbors, let alone your government. It simply can't be done in our increasingly digitized world. I am not willing to give up Google Maps, Facebook, Groupon, mobile phones, and electronic tax refunds. And whether I like them or not, Internet tracking, DRM, the mash-ups of public and private data, and high speed analytic software and hardware are here to stay.

The second is more hopeful. Whatever your stance on the correctness of the recent disclosure of US government secrets by WikiLeaks, it has clearly shown that even the world's preeminent military power is not immune to the transparency-inducing effects of ubiquitous computing. Not only is individual privacy being eroded, but so is big brother's ability to keep secrets (a friend to corrupt governments, criminals, and dictators throughout human history). Privacy erosion is a subset of secrecy erosion. My sincere hope is that the potential horrors enabled by the former will be outweighed by the horrors prevented by the light of the latter. And since I believe that the chances of our returning to our previous privacy norms is a pipe dream, we should all keep our fingers crossed that I am right.

But just in case I am not, here is one thing to remember from the book: "What happens on the Internet, Stays on the Internet."

Mary's Point of View

Well, our book is almost done—it's now in production phase and Terence and I are finished with most of the heavy writing (unless our editor has some additional thoughts!). In terms of time, it really has not been that long since we signed on to do it—less than six months from initial concept to publication date. In terms of thought and brain-power, well now, that's a very different story!

It has been a long, arduous, sometimes acrimonious (in the nicest possible way, of course) journey. You know, working for a small, privately held company means that even in the best of times, you already have multiple jobs so when you add writing a book on top of those, you tend to get a little fractured. This means that your family and friends may get a wee bit irritated with you because you simply do not have time and even when you do, you are usually talking about some aspect of privacy. So, to all my friends and family, thank you for being so understanding and for reading and reviewing our chapters!

When we started this process, we both thought that we could bring something interesting to the table. Between us, Terence and I represent different genders, different functions (marketing versus über geek/technologist/ceo), and a multitude of ethnicities. We come from very different places and have different worldviews—particularly when it comes to privacy. Although we both talk and blog about the topic a lot, it's safe to say that each of us has been known to say to the other, "You're missing the point." We figured that together, we could pretty much cover the privacy landscape and that our differing views might make for some interesting discussions. And they did.

What I didn't count on is how writing the book would affect my view of privacy. Now if you follow our blog, you are probably quite familiar where I stand on the privacy debate because I've posted about it quite often (see our blog at *http://blog.patternbuild ers.com/*). For those of you not familiar with my views, here's the short version:

- The U.S. needs more comprehensive privacy legislation and its needs to have some significant enforcement teeth.
- Anyone who collects and rents/sells personal information must always inform the user and all uses of data should be opt-in only.
- Privacy policies should be standardized and anything to do with privacy that is not standard should be explained, including specific third party uses, and offered as an opt-in.

Pretty simple huh? Except that privacy is not a simple topic. It's complicated and nuanced and there are so many facets to it. Then add in the fact that technology keeps giving us new and different ways to do pretty much anything online and that data has no boundaries but privacy regulations do, and it's enough to throw up your hands and say, "I surrender!"

I have to admit that when we started the book, I was pretty sure that I knew how it ended. There's so much of our personal information out there and we know very little about how it's being used, making the outlook on retaining one's privacy in the digital world pretty dismal. But I discovered that although the outlook might not be rosy, each one of us has control over what we do next.

It's a given that our personal information is out there (if you don't believe me, just spokeo (*http://www.spokeo.com/*) yourself) but we still have control over how much we add to it every time we do something on our Smartphone, iPad, laptop, or fill-in-the-blank-with-your favorite-device. So think about what level of privacy you would like to have online and then start making some decisions on what you are going to do from this day forward (and if you're happy with the status quo, keeping doing what you're doing). For me, it's this:

- No Facebook presence—I never had an account and have decided that I never will. And if you think this is just because Facebook is not "great" (to put it mildly) in the privacy department, you'd be wrong. I made a decision long ago to keep my personal life offline (my professional one is pretty much everywhere) and I am sticking to it.

- No doing business with companies who have egregious privacy violations—until they clean up their act and prove to me that they are once again on the straight and narrow.

- Doing business with companies who toe the privacy line by getting privacy certifications, building privacy into their products, or quickly responding (and fixing) privacy problems (because anyone can make a mistake).

- No putting personal photos and videos and anything else "personal" online. Hey, this is not for everyone but it's a rule I live by (and yes, family and friends give me a hard time about it, but they all do me the kindness of not including me in their Facebook pages, etc.).

- Being a privacy activist—if I don't like what's going on I am saying something about it on Twitter, on our blog, or in comments. The great thing about the world we live in today is that we can all be heard via social media.

Listen, there are things that we can do to mitigate our loss of privacy from using tools to simply not being so forthcoming online. We can give our business to those we trust looking for privacy seal guarantees (like TRUSTe (*http://www.truste.com/*)), or those who commit to a privacy code of conduct, or those who build privacy into their products (Privacy by Design (*http://privacybydesign.ca/*)). When companies behave badly, there are penalties that we (not just the courts) can apply—like no longer using a site or revoking our membership. Instead of throwing up my hands in defeat (as in there is no such thing as privacy in the digital world), I am more energized than ever before.

There's still time for our voices to be heard in this debate and there's still time for meaningful change but it's up to us, me, you, and everybody else, to start figuring out exactly what privacy means in the digital age and then how to, in the words of Tim Gunn on Project Runway: "Make it work."

When we finished the last chapter of the book, Terence and I had a long conversation about where we stood on privacy and I will share with you what I shared with him. Here's my dream (people looking for a startup idea, please take note): if Microsoft and Dartmouth college (*http://www.microsoft.com/presspass/presskits/photodna/*) can develop PhotoDNA to help remove images of child sexual exploitation from the Internet (this is an amazing story and if you haven't read about it before, go to that link because it has lots of information), then who's to say that five years down the road someone won't be able to come up with personal data DNA which will track where our data is from that point forward (and what it's being used for) all over the Internet? Then when we give our personal information out we will be able to see exactly what happens to it or in my scenario, pay some company $20/month to be the Equifax version of privacy (as in monitor and alert me when my privacy may have been violated).

Now for those of you who say it will never happen, think about all the devices you now use to power through your life. Many of them did not exist five years ago and most of them did not exist ten years ago. Who's to say what the privacy landscape looks like in five years? There's one thing that I am sure of: I'll be keeping an eye out to see what happens next!

About the Authors

Terence Craig is the CEO and CTO of PatternBuilders, a "big data" analytics services and solution provider that helps organizations across industries understand and improve their operations with advanced analytics. Terence has an extensive background in building, implementing, and selling analytically-driven enterprise and SaaS applications across such diverse domains as enterprise resource planning (ERP), professional services automation (PSA), and semi-conductor process control in both public and private companies. With over 20 years of experience in executive and technical management roles with leading-edge technology companies, Terence brings a unique and innovative view of what is needed—from both an operational and technology perspective—to build a world class hosted analytics platform designed to improve companies' and organizations' profitability and efficiencies. He is also a frequent speaker, blogger, and "commenter" on technology, startups, analytics, data security, and data privacy ethics and policy.

Mary is the VP of marketing for PatternBuilders, a "big data" analytics services and solutions company. She is an innovative executive with more than 20 years of experience in the high-tech industry. When it comes to marketing, she has, in her own words, "been there, done that, and often, with little or no budget." Our translation: Mary understands how to develop and implement strategic program initiatives that span marketing disciplines—ranging from the traditional corporate and marketing fields to the latest developments in digital marketing (yes, much more descriptive and far less interesting than her own words). Through her work at Brio Technology (now Hyperion) and NONSTOP Solutions (now Manhattan Associates), Mary also brings a deep understanding of supply chain management issues as well as the use of business intelligence tools in data warehousing and analytic application efforts. Mary is a frequent white paper contributor, an editor of many reference manuals, user manuals, and other publications, and a blogger on diverse topics such as big data and analytics from a technology and business perspective, data security, data privacy, and marketing in the digital age.

Get even more for your money.

The information you need, when and where you need it.

With Safari Books Online, you can:

Access the contents of thousands of technology and business books

- Quickly search over 7000 books and certification guides
- Download whole books or chapters in PDF format, at no extra cost, to print or read on the go
- Copy and paste code
- Save up to 35% on O'Reilly print books
- **New!** Access mobile-friendly books directly from cell phones and mobile devices

Stay up-to-date on emerging topics before the books are published

- Get on-demand access to evolving manuscripts.
- Interact directly with authors of upcoming books

Explore thousands of hours of video on technology and design topics

- Learn from expert video tutorials
- Watch and replay recorded conference sessions

Spreading the knowledge of innovators   safari.oreilly.com

CPSIA information can be obtained at www.ICGtesting.com
Printed in the USA
LVOW121720041011

249065LV00003B/18/P